The Yoga Mindset

The Yoga Mindset
Change Your Mindset, Change Your Life
Michelle Gervais-Bryan

Published by Game Changer Publishing

Cover Design by Margaret Bryan, Graphic Designer,
https://www.behance.net/maggiebryandesigns
Mandala Illustration purchased at www.shutterstock.com

ISBN: 978-1-7370407-0-5

www.PublishABestSellingBook.com

DEDICATION

Every so often, a very special person passes through this world who not only sees the best in everyone they meet, but also takes great joy in helping those people grow, advance, and live out their life purpose. This person operates from a place of divine love, expecting neither praise nor payback, and they are a gift to the world. This person is none other than my extraordinary husband, Dan. My love, thank you for showing me how to live, laugh and love so well, and for perpetually restoring my faith in both God and humanity by simply being you. You are my hero. This book is lovingly dedicated to you, first and foremost, and to a few other beautiful souls that I've been privileged to know, love, and learn from in this lifetime.

To my brave and beautiful mother, Carol, thank you for surviving, for keeping me, and for always whispering into my eyes, ears, and heart that I am enough.

To my creative and talented sister, Alisa, thank you for being my first, best little sis, playmate, and forever best friend.

To my feisty great aunts, Emma and Caroline, thank you for helping me see God in everything.

To my crazy fun aunt, Sharon, thank you for loving the small broken things of the world.

To my faithful stepfather, KJ, thank you for caring for widows and orphans in their distress.

To my best friend, Tonya, thank you for opening your heart and home when I needed it most.

To my amazing children, Joseph, Maggie, and Samuel, the light of my eyes and the song in my heart. You are enough and you can do anything you set your mind to doing. I love you, I'm always in your corner. You got this!

You've *all* taught me how to live the best version of myself and my life and I am eternally grateful.

DOWNLOAD YOUR FREE GIFTS

Read This First

Just to say thanks for buying and reading my book, I would like to give you three bonus gifts for FREE, no strings attached!

To Download Now, Visit:

www.TheYogaMindsetBook.com/FreeGifts

The Yoga Mindset

Change Your Mindset, Change Your Life

Michelle Gervais-Bryan

Game Changer
PUBLISHING
www.PublishABestSellingBook.com

I am not what happened to me,
I am what I choose to become.

Carl Jung

Foreword

"I saw the angel in the marble and carved until I set him free."

Michelangelo

In the summer of 2016, Michelle Gervais-Bryan presented me with a massive boulder, hewn from the caves of her life, along with a request to help her release the angel that was stuck inside.

I recognize a good story when I hear it, and this one hooked me immediately. It needed to be told, but I could see that she needed some guidance on how and where to begin.

With great care and precision, I guided her in the placement of both the mallet and the chisel, from one manuscript to the next, until all that needed to be subtracted was removed and only the essence of what was necessary remained.

With the final blow of the mallet, we both stepped back and marveled at the breathtaking masterpiece that was always there, just below the surface. That same sense of breakthrough to the best version of your life awaits in the pages of this book.

We are all in this thing called 'life' together, and though it's not always easy, there are three timeless secrets that can make it a masterpiece.

The Yoga Mindset is the key to unlocking those secrets, and Michelle will be your guide each step of the way.

With the wonder of a child, the eye of an artist and the precision of a sculptor, she will guide you in the placement of both the mallet and the chisel on the rock of *your* life, until all that needs to be subtracted is removed, and only the essence of what is necessary, and a masterpiece, remains.

With whole-hearted enthusiasm, I recommend this book to anyone who knows, deep down inside, that they were meant for so much more, and are ready to begin the journey to true freedom.

@SammieB, Founder & Editor
The Cellar Door Collective

Table of Contents

Introduction

There is an ancient Japanese legend that tells the story of a mighty shogun warrior who broke his favorite tea bowl and sent it away for repairs. When it was returned to him, and he saw the unsightly staples holding the broken pieces together, he was displeased. Hoping to restore it to its former beauty, he sent it out to a craftsman with a request for a more elegant solution.

The craftsman knew exactly what to do. He used a new repair technique that would not only restore the bowl to its original beauty, but also increase its value. He carefully joined all the broken pieces back together with a lacquer resin mixed with precious gold. When it was returned to the warrior, and he saw the streaks of gold running throughout the bowl telling its story, he was pleased.

This new method of repair became known as *kintsugi* or "golden joinery." It expresses the Japanese philosophy of ascribing great value to things, not based on their perfection but their imperfection.

This simple, but profound, story reminds me that we are all kintsugi to one degree or another. Some of us are like the bowl at the start of the story, not yet impacted by the world and still in our original form. Others are like the broken bowl, feeling shattered into fragments as a result of some unanticipated life experience. Some of us are in the process of mending the cracks of those fragments with precious gold. Others, feeling restored and whole again, have returned to their purpose in life as perfectly imperfect vessels.

Of all the possible *kintsugi* stages, where would you say *you* are at this moment in your life? What's your kintsugi story?

My *kintsugi* story begins one degree north of the equator in tropical Singapore. My family and I had just been transferred there after several years of living and working in Japan, and we were in the chaotic throes of unpacking our personal baggage and setting up our new home. Singapore's hot and balmy temperatures were both a shock to the system and a mirror image of the hot mess I felt like on the inside. Not quite ready to deal with all of my own "personal and deeper baggage," I instead found a job and started working. I was offered a position as an architect with a cutting-edge Singaporean architectural design studio, and I was completely and happily distracted from all of my deeper issues.

I was living the expat life and loving it, but deep down, I knew that I was restless in my spirit. I knew that I would eventually need to take a deep dive into all of it, but I didn't really know where or how to begin, and I surely didn't have the time since I was now so busy working. Singapore would eventually show me the way.

At 6 am, before the official hustle and bustle of the emerald city begins, a committed group of expats, and Singaporeans, gather on the second floor of a dimly lit row house in Chinatown that has been converted into a hot yoga studio. With an outdoor temperature of 87 degrees and what feels like 100 percent humidity, plus an intentionally-set indoor temperature of 100 degrees, the studio is a steamy sauna. It's also a grand example of British architecture during the roaring 20s, with soaring ceilings at least twenty feet high, punctuated by a couple of lazy palm leaf-shaped ceiling fans. The windows are equally tall and their shutters are open wide to the street below. The sheer white curtain, framing the windows, shimmer as the fans sift the rising hot air back down towards the floor and the sweltering participants. The thin black yoga mats are aligned so tightly that they are almost touching on all four sides, and most everyone is sitting, or lying down, on their mats trying to acclimate to the heat and the negligible personal space. Most eyes are closed, and words are spoken in hushed tones. The collective breath moves slowly and deeply.

Since the sun has not yet risen, the light in the room is minimal at best, but in the semi-darkness, I spy an open mat at the back of the room. "Thank God it's in the back," I think to myself, and I walk over to settle in. I'd taken, and taught, traditional yoga classes, but this was my first "hot" yoga class. My neighbor, also a new expat in Singapore, had invited me, explaining that it would be life-altering. As a fitness instructor and personal trainer, I was interested, but I didn't really buy into the whole life-altering bit. Nonetheless, I was new to the area and feeling ready to connect, so I accepted the offer.

As I was sitting still on my mat, beads of sweat started rolling down my spine. A slight discomfort set in, and I began to wonder about the wisdom of my decision. I'd suffered from panic attacks for several years, for reasons I still couldn't explain, and the setting was not exactly ideal for someone prone to panic attacks. I was starting to feel some anxiety rising up in me.

"Not again," I sighed to myself. I started talking myself down from the ledge. "Breathe, you are safe. Look around. No one is harming you. It's just as hot as Hades," I told myself. My anxiety was still rising. "Maybe I just needed a fresh breath of air," I thought. Gazing over my shoulder at the clock, I realized that I still had time to spare and slipped out quickly. In the open and much cooler lobby, I inhaled deeply, exhaled and relaxed. I reminded myself again that all was well and that I could walk out, at any time, if I wanted, or needed, to do so. That did the trick and I stepped back into the sauna.

Everything was exactly as I left it, except for a new, and subtle, smell of perspiration now weaving itself into the air, as I made my way back to my mat. Like standing in the gentle foam at the edge of the ocean, the hushed sounds of the deep and focused breathing throughout the room helped to calm me further. Gently breaking through the surf, in an enchanting accent that was not quite English and not quite Singaporean, the yoga instructor calmly greeted everyone, introduced himself, and invited us to stand together to begin. With our hands to our hearts in prayer position, we inhaled, exhaled, and like the ocean, we began to flow.

For one hour, the instructor guided us through a series of synchronized poses and breathwork, peppered with moments of stillness and contemplation. There wasn't any music, only his voice, rising and falling, urging everyone to find the fullest expression in each of the poses: to reach a little farther, to root a little deeper, and to exhale a little more expansively amidst the now rising waves of ocean breathing.

At some point, I lost track of the edges of myself in relation to the others. It felt like we were all one massive wave moving together in a series of sweeping ebbs and flows of both breath and presence. We reached up, we folded forward, we swayed, we twisted, we opened our hearts, we closed our eyes, we inhaled, we exhaled, we focused, we balanced, we inverted, we extended, we soared. It felt like a choreographed routine on Broadway that we all somehow knew by heart. As we neared the end of the hour, we held the final pinnacle pose: Dancer Pose.

As if I'd just finished a marathon, I was drenched, breathing heavily and exhilarated. To steady myself, I recovered my focal point in the distance and inhaled a slow deep breath. Standing as still as a statue, another thick bead of sweat ran from my temple to my cheek, in what seemed like slow motion. As that bead of sweat fell from my chin to the floor, I exhaled, and time slowed to a crawl.

The high tide of ocean breath in the room receded to a whisper, and I felt like I was floating somewhere between the earth and the sky; a kite without a string, hovering above everyone and everything. Time was meaningless. There was just the awareness of the stillness of my body, the breathlessness of my lungs, and the vibration of my heart pumping blood throughout my body. I was completely aware of the people in the room, the sounds on the street below, the city, the world, and the feeling of connectedness to all of it, all at once, past, present and future. The sun was slowly rising and filtering in through the windows, illuminating everyone and everything.

In the light of that moment, I was finally able to see the pieces of my life in a completely new way. I finally understood how they all fit together, and I saw them telling their story in beautiful lines of gold. It was a breathtaking mosaic. Like the shogun warrior, seeing the mosaic of my life tell its story in lines of gold, I was very pleased. I smiled as a deep and much needed rest washed over me, and I came out of Dancer Pose.

The yoga class came to an end and the instructor closed by inviting us all to stand together once again. With my hands to my heart, I bowed my head and smiled when I realized that I felt full of more love, peace, and joy than I ever thought possible. I was fully present and connected to myself and others, for the first time in a long time. It was as if my spirit, split three ways between the past, present and future, finally caught up with my body all at the same time.

Not quite touching the ground, I floated out of the studio, thanked my friend for the invitation, and enthusiastically confirmed that *"yes, it was everything you said it would be and more."* In fact, it was so life-altering that I never suffered another panic attack again.

Life continued to slam into me, a continuous and guaranteed hazard of being alive and in this world, but instead of being completely shattered by each new impact, I started to reframe them as unanticipated upgrades and personal growth opportunities. I chose to flow with them. I chose to look for the lessons in every challenge, so that I could get through it as quickly as possible. I chose to adjust my sail and harness the force of the winds from various life storms to propel me forward to a better life. I wish I could say that I have flowed perfectly in the face of every challenge since that yoga class, but that would not be true. I'm still human.

I still get upset. I still wonder why things happen the way they do. I'm still careless with my words and actions. I'm still a work in progress. Practice doesn't make perfect. Practice makes progress. I'm getting better at flowing with life "as it is" and progressing all the time.

The real difference now is my mindset. I have a constant, deep peace and calm, where I used to be a steamy hot mess. It's a peace that passes all understanding, and it sustains me when nothing else makes sense. It's far beyond the reach of any challenge that I may face. It's far beyond the reach of this world or human thinking.

That shift in thinking, that new mindset, what I call The Yoga Mindset, was a game changer for me. It helped me to see that what felt like life always happening *to* me was actually life happening *for* me. Don't get me wrong. The storms of life were still devastating. I don't mean to minimize the reality of pain and suffering. It's very real. In the most extreme cases, where someone is a danger to themselves or others, it is not just real, it can be horrible and life-threatening. In those situations, it is strongly recommended to seek help as quickly as possible.

Though we can't always control all the circumstances of our lives, we can always choose our response to those circumstances and the stories we tell ourselves about them. They can be disempowering stories and keep us stuck in the past or unforgiveness, or they can be empowering stories that liberate us to move forward. Which do you prefer? To be disempowered or empowered? It's really all up to you. It's all in your mindset.

I've carried the gift of *The Yoga Mindset* for several years now, and it has made all the difference in my life. My hope is that it might be a game changer for you, too. So, like my dear friend, who invited me to that yoga class in Singapore, I would like to invite *you* to a yoga class in the pages of the Yoga Mindset.

No, you don't have to be super flexy, or do pretzel yoga, to get the full benefit of this book. You do, however, need a flexible mind, open to applying the seven secret alignment principles of one of the most fundamental poses in a yoga class, Mountain Pose, to both your body and your mind. Additionally, we'll dive into seven principles of the Chakra system, an ancient system of health and wellness, still in use today around the world. I don't pretend to be an expert on the chakras, but I invite you to learn about them and use them as a guide to help you start, or go deeper into your practice, or to simply get 'unstuck' in life.

The seven key areas that we'll consider include:

1. Your relationship to your family of origin specifically, but in the absence of a connection to your family of origin, it could also be any other group you consider your 'family' or your 'tribe', in

general, such as a military group, school group, sports team, church group, yoga group, etc.

2. Your relationships with other people outside your family such as friends, colleagues, romantic interests, etc.
3. Your relationship with yourself.
4. Your ability to give and receive love.
5. Your ability to speak and be heard.
6. Your ability to see and be seen.
7. Your ability to know and be known by the Creator.

Some people refer to the Creator of everything as God, Jesus, the Universe, the Divine, Nature, Source, and many other names. For the purposes of this book, since I was raised in the Christian faith, I will refer to the Creator as God.

No matter your faith, of lack thereof, this book is designed to be a seven-day challenge for anyone and everyone. The recommendation is to work your way through the book, one chapter per day over seven days. Some people will follow this proposed timeline, but others may prefer to take it a bit slower. All approaches are okay. Your experience will be unique to you and your needs, so decide the timeline that best serves you. Whether seven days, seven weeks, or seven months, we'll all eventually meet at the top of the mountain, and the view may be life-altering for you, too.

For this journey, you will be traveling light. You'll need a journal, a pen or pencil, a yoga mat, a designated space to practice, and the courage to take a deep dive into your life as you practice the Yoga Mindset Formula daily. If you don't have a mat, a pen or pencil or even paper, you are still welcome to take this challenge.

If, at any time on this journey, you find anything too challenging to address independently, for any reason whatsoever, it is recommended to try speaking to a trusted family member, friend, therapist, or doctor, who can help you deal with any deeper issues. On this journey, your job will be to do four things:

1. Observe and document, without judgment, the structure, from foundation to the roof, of your life.
2. Look for the lessons in every crack, misalignment and broken fragment.
3. Flip the script on any disempowering stories you may have been telling yourself.
4. Create new and empowering stories in lines of gold, and move forward in life.

Some suggestions before each day's journey:

1. Set out everything you will need the night before.
2. Read the chapter the day or night before.
3. Read all the questions the day or night before.

If you can do all of this before the next morning, when you wake up you won't have to think about, or do, anything to prepare for the 15 minute practice. Everything will be ready to go. If you can't get to all of it the night before, you can still show up and reap the benefits! Once you are in your space, set your timer.

Some options for your timing could include setting an alarm on your clock for 15 minutes total, for five minutes at a time manually, or for 3- five minute segments if you have a smartphone. With the first option, you'll have to keep a close eye on the clock and transition at the five and ten minute mark. With the second option, you'll lose a bit of time resetting the clock manually for an additional 5 minutes between the three segments of the practice. With the last option, you don't have to do much in the transitions except to listen for the alarm. All options work, so depending on your situation, decide which is the best setup for you. Then, get ready to move, meditate and manifest the best version of your life.

Why Move? — We move because our amazing bodies were designed to move and breathe and operate at peak levels daily. There will always be excuses to avoid movement. As a personal trainer, I feel like I've heard them all. They usually show up first thing in the morning. I'm too tired, too cold, too sore, too short on time, too short on interest, and that is just the tip of the iceberg. The path of least resistance is always compelling in the moment, but it rarely helps anyone move forward towards their goals in the long term.

So, get ready to flip the switch on your thinking about daily movement. It's still the best medicine for everybody with manifold positive side effects. No need to run a marathon. Just set aside five minutes for movement every morning for seven days. Do it for yourself so that you can be, and do, all you hope for in your life. You can move just about anywhere. It could be in your bedroom, in your basement, or in front of a mirror. Wherever you decide to create your space for movement, commit to five minutes of movement every morning.

While any time of day will do for practicing the Yoga Mindset Formula, mornings are recommended as it's the time when you can set the tone and focus of your whole day. Trouble getting out of bed? I heartily recommend Mel Robbins' clever launching trick.

When the alarm goes off, while still in bed, count backward 5...4...3...2...1... and then, like a rocket, visualize launching yourself out of bed and then do it. Next, set your timer, and plug into the power of the Yoga Mindset Formula for 15 minutes to capture the day before it even begins.

Why Meditate? — This is the fruit of your movement, and it is the powerhouse of the Yoga Mindset Formula. As *Anatomy Trains* author Thomas W. Myers declares, "Exercise from below helps us up above." We meditate after we move because it's the next step in the process of enhancing the mind-body connection. Where movement delivers oxygenated blood to our muscles and organs, so that we can think and move more effectively, meditation delivers focused thinking on something, like an inspirational quote, an object in the distance, or your breath, to calm an often scattered mind. In the yoga world, the mind is occasionally referred to as the monkey mind, swinging from the past to the future but rarely staying in the present for very long.

Meditation, also referred to as prayer in the Christian world, quiets the monkey mind. I can't tell you how many times I've lain awake in bed at night, rehearsing all the things that occurred that day, in addition to all that I'll do the next day. Meanwhile, my husband is millimeters away from me in bed. He's warm, breathing and alive, and I'm a million miles away, swinging from the past and the future in my mind. Sound familiar? If so, you are in good company. Commit to the Yoga Mindset meditation segment of the formula for an additional five minutes every morning after you move, and notice if you move through your day with an improved level of focus, presence, and calm intention. Next, we'll manifest.

Why Manifest? — This is the life-altering fruit of your meditation. This is the part of the formula where you will proactively visualize, and co-create, the best version of yourself and your life, as you define it. These last five minutes of the Yoga Mindset Formula have the potential to change the entire trajectory of your life. To get the most out of these last five minutes, give yourself permission to dream BIG! Ask yourself what you really want in your life. Imagine the ideal version of yourself and your life and then see and feel yourself there. Let those feelings run through you. What would that life look, feel, sound, taste and be like? Can you imagine it? Then think about the changes and steps that may need to occur in your life in order to move in the direction of that dream.

Here's the bottom line: You are the author of your life story, and you have the power to flip the script of your life at any time. So, don't waste any more time replaying the negative and disempowering stories in your head about the past. Dare to tell yourself new and empowering stories in the manifestation segment of the Yoga Mindset Formula every day.

In addition to this seven-day journey, you can also join me for a FREE 3 Day Yoga Mindset Challenge online, which will show you exactly how to move, meditate and manifest for 15 minutes a day together. To join this challenge, sign up here: www.mosaicconcepts.com/yogachallenge

Tired of feeling like a fragmented, broken hot mess, watching everyone else move forward while you feel stuck in life? Learn how to mend the fragments of your life with precious lines of gold and start living your life to the fullest as a perfectly imperfect vessel. Learn how to harness the energy of those life storms to make you better, not bitter. Learn how to celebrate and display your life scars. You are a once-in-a-million, magnificent and unique mosaic life. You have a purpose to fulfill in the very short amount of time you've been given. Is there anything more important?

CHAPTER 1

I Am

"I should like to ask you:
Does your childhood seem far off?
Do the days when you sat at your mother's knee seem days of very long ago?
Twenty years back, yes; at this time of my life, no.
For as I draw closer and closer to the end,
I travel in the circle, nearer and nearer to the beginning.
It seems to be one of kind smoothings and preparings of the way..."

Charles Dickens, *A Tale of Two Cities*

With the foil encrusted rabbit ears on our TV finally adjusted, *Yoga with Lilias* came into view. She was a tall, thin yoga instructor with long brown hair braided down one side of her body. She was wearing a black, long-sleeved, scooped-neck leotard, and she was the embodiment of the 70s "yoga as exercise" movement. At the age of twenty-four, my beautiful mother, with equally long black hair, and I, were utterly captivated by the magic of Lilias' soft voice, slow movements, and this new thing called yoga. I personally felt like I was watching *Romper Room* with Lilias looking at me through the magic looking glass.

We had so much fun on the floor of our living room, breathing deeply and mirroring Lilias to the best of our ability. I was a five-year-old rubber band, and my mom was pretty flexible, too. We laughed a lot at ourselves during those brief forays into flexibility, and the joy of our time together far outweighed the fact that we were living well below the poverty line, in the tiniest of apartments, high above a busy highway in southern Maryland. I have a few other blurry and scattered memories of my life with my parents during my younger years, but mostly I just remember those yoga sessions with my mom. As Gary Chapman so concisely stated in *The 5 Love Languages*, "Love begins, or should begin, at home." To have seen my mom so light and happy filled my soul, and it still does to this day. I had no idea that we were poor because we had so much love, and we had each other. Our life was simple, and to me, perfect. It was the mirror image of the lyrics to the Sonny and Cher song, "I Got You Babe."

My Dad landed a manual typesetting job right out of high school with *The Washington Post*, so he was gone most days. Having gotten pregnant during her senior year, my mom didn't have any job skills or college training, so we both stayed home together. When we weren't doing yoga, we played. That simple act of play was significant for both of us. For me, it was building my sense of connection, body awareness, and self-confidence. For her, it was a chance to experience the childhood that was stolen from her at a very young age.

Her father was a U.S. Marine who fought in both Guadalcanal and the Korean War. Between his rough upbringing on a moonshine farm, somewhere in the backwoods of Alabama, and the horrors of war, I suspect he was in dire need of mental health support when he finally returned home.

Unfortunately, support for the military returning from war in the 50s was nothing like it is today. Folks just didn't talk about things like PTSD back then. If there was trauma, dysfunction, or any other sort of issue in a family, it was kept in the family. Apparently, he had good days and bad days. When it was a good day, despite no formal training, he was able to hold down positions as critical as a foreman on construction sites. When he was having a bad day, however, he had trouble with everything. As a result, he was frequently out of work, depressed, and drinking. With kids to feed and a mortgage to pay, my grandmother had no choice but to find a full-time job, leaving him home alone to "take care" of the kids.

According to my mom, while her mother was at work, she was abused by her father in every conceivable way. She was only seven years old. She repeatedly begged her mother, and the police, for help and protection, but neither came to her aid. Her feelings of abandonment, on top of the repetitive physical and mental abuse by her father, took a profound mental toll on her. The nightmare finally came to an end when at the age of sixteen, my mom stabbed her father in the leg in self-defense. Half naked and hysterical, she escaped from the house and ran to a nearby drugstore.

A compassionate woman at the register of the drugstore took my mother's pleas for help seriously and quickly hid her under the counter.

After denying that she was there and arguing with my grandfather about whether he was, or wasn't, going to purchase anything, he left in a rage. The saleswoman called the police as soon as he was gone. They shuttled my mom to the station for a report where she would detail everything that had occurred that night and all the years prior. That was all the information they needed. She was transferred to a shelter temporarily for her protection. Her father was arrested and taken to jail to await trial.

On the day of the trial, my mom took the stand to read that list of offenses in front of the judge, jury, and her parents. She said it was the hardest thing she ever did. She said that she remembers the jury catching their breath in shock as she read off the offenses. He was found guilty and ended up in the federal penitentiary for sexual assault of a minor, among many other charges.

With him out of the picture, my mom could finally move forward with her life. Long-term therapy was desperately needed, but not really an option financially, so she just did the best she could. Eventually, she started dating a senior during her junior year in high school, and eventually, they fell in love. They married right after her graduation, and five months later, I was born. You can do the math.

I was a "love child" of the 60s, and my parents were hipsters obsessed with the Beatles. Hence, my name. With this groovy combo of parents, yoga felt like a normal and natural offshoot of our lives, and I cherish those moments as sacred. From the age of five to seven, my mother and I spent many glorious days in our living room practicing yoga together with Lilias. At the end of each day, my Dad would burst through the door smelling of both grease and ink, and my sister and I would attack and wrestle him to the floor where non-stop wrestling, tickling, and giggling would ensue. He always let us think we were pinning him down.

We were a happy family of four, but in December of 1973, everything changed. In a time when seatbelts were optional, my father was mortally wounded by a drunk driver in a head-on collision. In an instant, our lives were changed forever.

My mom didn't share any of the details with us, but I remember being very aware that something was wrong. One day our father was with us, and the next day he was "sick and in the hospital," according to my mom. Years later, as an adult, I would find out that he wasn't sick. He was brain dead and on a ventilator for life support. I'd also learn that after their meager savings account was spent on medical bills, and the doctors had told my mom that there was nothing else they could do, she had to make the gut-wrenching decision to remove him from life support. Before that moment, she took us to see him one last time.

We took the stairs deep into the basement of the hospital, where the air hung so still and stale that you could see the specks of dust floating on the few beams of sunlight entering the space. After passing several people that seemed to be sleeping without breathing, I saw my Dad. He was propped up on his right side in a small bed by several strategically placed pillows, and he was staring at me without moving or blinking. Since he couldn't blink, tears were continuously running down his cheeks. While I thought that was strange, I thought it was even stranger to see that the left side of his head was somehow different. Feeling scared and confused, I leaned into my mom and buried my face into her coat. Looking up at her, in a whisper, I asked, "Why is Daddy staring at me like that?" I don't remember what she said. I just remember that seeing my Dad staring at me without blinking, moving, or saying anything was unsettling. At some point, though, I remembered that he was still my Dad, and the unconditional love of a child kicked in. I started talking to him as if nothing had changed, and I remember feeling like he saw, heard, and understood everything I was saying about my day, mom, and my three-year-old little sister. I felt like we were together again, and it seemed like all was well in the world.

The next day, my mom told us that he had gone to heaven and that he would not be coming home again. I didn't fully understand what was happening or what she meant, but I remember feeling even more scared and confused when I heard the words. I just wanted him to come home again. I just wanted our life to go back to normal, but nothing would ever be normal again. I was seven years old.

Widowed at twenty-six, without a job or savings, and two young girls, ages seven and three to feed, my mother was lost in a fog of confusion, grief, and despair. A thick, heavy sorrow seeped into our home and hearts as I'd listen to her howl through the night. Night, after night, after night, she just kept crying and cursing God.

Things were strange at school, too. The teachers and students started whispering about me from a distance, and they started treating me like I'd somehow become fragile overnight. The teachers didn't push me academically, compared to all the other students, and my grades plummeted. Those feelings of separation made me feel so disconnected, different, and alone. In my frustration, I started getting into fights at school and ended up in the principal's office. I wasn't doing so well. None of us were doing very well.

With two kids to feed and rent still due every month, my mom had no choice but to find a job to make ends meet. The yoga and the playtime stopped. Early mornings at before-school care, followed by long days of feeling alone and misunderstood in school, followed by even longer afternoons in after-school care, plus one respiratory infection after another, was the new rhythm of our lives. There were occasional moments of sunshine, however. Sometimes, my sister and I were given some leftover S&H Green Stamps, and those days kept me afloat!

Random men would pass in and out of our home and get very friendly with my mom. About a year later, however, my mom told us that the man driving the car that day would be our new Dad soon. I remember feeling confused about that statement because I only had one Dad. Even though he was in heaven, he was still my real Dad. I didn't understand. Nothing more was said about it, though, and I somehow understood that it was not a topic open for discussion. They married soon afterward, and just as quickly, we were all baptized as Catholics. My sister and I were legally adopted, and our birth name of Yezek was stricken from all official records.

With a new Dad, a new last name, and a faith that I knew nothing about, we moved to a distant and unknown place called Houston, Texas. My mom seemed happy again. Our lives evened out into a new rhythm, but I sensed that our new Dad didn't really like me or my sister very much.

My mom became pregnant quickly after their marriage, but lost the baby at birth. Devastated, my stepdad withdrew emotionally and dove into his work while my mom spiraled downward once again. This time, however, it would be years before she would come back to us. Like a silent earthquake beneath the ocean floor, the fault line of her heart and mind completely gave way when her baby died. The resulting emotional tsunami overtook her so quickly that no one could reach her.

In and out of mental hospitals, she was overmedicated, undermedicated, and self-medicated for weeks or months at a time. My stepdad, sister, and I learned how to survive with the new normal of an absent mother suffering from mental illness. None of us saw it coming, and none of us were prepared to handle it. Like people suddenly trapped under the rubble and debris in the aftermath of an earthquake, we just kept reaching out our hands in the dark, feeling for a possible passageway to fresh air and sunlight. We took it one cautious and measured step at a time, praying the rubble wouldn't cave in and crush us completely, too.

We barely knew our new "father," but we were all of a sudden home alone with him. With mom out of the picture, it became very clear that he not only didn't like us, but also felt like we couldn't do anything right and he let us know it routinely. As a result, we tried to avoid him as much as possible. This didn't bode well for our budding confidence or a much needed father-daughter relationship, especially at that time in our lives. Our hearts were sad, anxious, and empty, whether mom was home or not, and life went on this way for years as my sister and I self-parented while we watched their marriage struggle under the pressure of it all.

Fast forward to when I was sixteen years old, with my parents arguing in their bedroom late one school night. Trying, impossibly, to go to sleep, I heard something that I'd never heard before: a gunshot.

I jumped out of bed and burst through their locked bedroom door to find my stepdad standing frozen at the foot of the bed with a gun in his hand. Fearing the worst, I looked slowly to the right over my shoulder and was relieved when I saw my mom, alive and hunched over on the edge of her side of the bed. She was surrounded by a massive splatter of blood on the wall behind her, and she was whimpering quietly, but she was alive. I moved closer and saw a stream of blood seep through her fingers as she gripped her shoulder. "Call 911," I yelled at my dad! He snapped out of his trance and made the call. I turned back to my mom, who was now rocking back and forth and crying in pain.

I gently pressed a towel to her shoulder and asked her what happened. In her drunken stupor, she told me that she tried to shoot herself in the heart, but that Dad slapped the gun away just as she was about to pull the trigger. She said the bullet hit her shoulder instead of her heart the moment he slapped her hand away. Horrified and confused by what she was saying, I asked her why she would *ever* do such a thing!

She paused, stared about a thousand miles away, through and past me, and said nothing. With tears now falling down my face, as the adrenaline subsided, I asked again, "Mom, why would you do that?" "Why would you leave us?" "Don't you love us enough to stay?" "Don't you know that *we* need you here?" Again, she stared right through me and said, "I just felt like I didn't have anything left to live for," and then she burst into tears. I heard what she was saying, but in my heart, it somehow translated into "I was not enough of a reason for my mom to keep living." I could hardly breathe.

The paramedics rushed through the bedroom door, and I stepped back quickly. Everything was happening in slow motion, as if on a movie screen. My mom was placed on the stretcher, and oxygen was administered along with some drugs. My step dad was talking to the paramedics about what happened, and from a distance, I felt like I saw things as they actually were for the first time.

My father was the vice president of a successful oil company in Houston, Texas, in the 80s. He drove a high-end sports car, and there was a Rolex on every wrist in the house. We had incredible financial stability, lived in one of the nicest houses, in one of the best neighborhoods, in one of the best school districts, yet we were struggling as a family. In the material world of the 80s, we had it all, and yet we seemed to have little of what mattered most. To make matters worse, for the first time in my life, I felt abandoned by my mother.

Following the stretcher to the ambulance in front of our house, I looked around our cul-de-sac to see several neighbors in robes and pajamas all huddled together in front of their houses, looking on from a distance. I felt like that little girl in elementary school again with everyone whispering about me. I wanted to disappear.

Sitting in the front passenger seat of the ambulance, staring into the darkness and watching the dashed center lines of the road whisk by, I wondered if we would ever be happy as a family. The driver tried to start a conversation with me, but it fell flat. I just sat quietly looking into the darkness, thinking about the first seven years of my life when we had nothing and everything.

I wondered to myself, *Why this? Why us? Why was everything always so difficult in our lives?* I wanted answers, but my mom was not available or able to help me connect the dots. So, I started asking my aunts and uncles questions about their childhood. Eventually, from their fragments of stories, that I could see cost them to share as they were not that different from hers, the pieces of the puzzle started to come together.

Raised with five other siblings, in a shack without electricity, running water, air conditioning, or heat, by bootlegging parents, deep in the backwoods of Alabama, my grandfather didn't have a very stable foundation to build his life upon. One of his children once told me that it was so bad in the shack where he grew up that bats hung from the ceiling. I suspect that the challenges of his childhood combined with the trauma of war created those profound negative ripple effects in his life, his mind, his marriage, and the lives of his children. Those ripples continue to flow through the generations, but they appear to affect everyone differently. Some struggle with low self-esteem, anger management, communication challenges, depression and divorce, while others struggle with alcohol abuse, drug addiction, poor physical health and mental illness. Still others, with extraordinary grit, seem to have broken free from the ripples, and the cycle of poverty and abuse, but they are few.

When I consider all that I have experienced personally and observed in the generations of the family, I am more convinced than ever that the role of a parent, or guardian, and in this case, the role of a father, is of the utmost importance in the life of a child. The foundation that a parent, or guardian, sets beneath the life of a child will have long-term positive or negative consequences for generations. What ripples were created in your life as a child through words or actions? What ripples are you creating in your children's lives?

Parents aren't perfect, believe me, as a parent, I know this to be true. We all do the best we can, and at least now, if support is needed, there is no shame in reaching out. It's the sanest and smartest thing you can do if you are feeling overwhelmed as a parent. There is no greater joy, and no greater challenge, than to parent, and it is so worth the effort, but sometimes we need help. Asking for help from a trusted friend, parent or professional is not a sign of weakness as a parent, quite the contrary. It is a sign of profound strength.

While most of the consequences in my mom's life were negative at the hands of her troubled father, there were also some amazingly positive results. It created a profound resiliency and strength in her that may have never been there otherwise.

She found her courage, voice, and confidence at sixteen years of age when she decided that enough was enough. She stood up for herself when no one else would. She testified against her father and went on to stand up for others in difficult situations, as well. She cared for the hurting and helped to feed the poor. She understood all of these life experiences intimately and, as a result, was able to authentically relate to and effectively help others in similar situations. She made and continues to make the world a better place in spite of what she experienced and endured. She could have easily played the role of a victim her whole life, and admittedly, she had every right, but that would not have helped her to move forward to the better life she dreamed of for herself.

Instead, she chose to work with psychologists and psychiatrists to recover her mental stability, her identity and self-worth and to flip the script on the disempowering stories that she had been telling herself for years. She replaced them with empowered stories fueled by the lessons learned during those unimaginable years of abuse. The very thing that was meant to destroy her actually made her stronger and fueled her towards the best version of herself and the best version of her life.

Despite everything that she experienced, she chose to tell herself that she was still of inestimable value and that she had something important to offer to the world. She called abuse what it was, but she also looked for the lessons in all of it, to help her become better not bitter. She declared that she had every right to be, to be in the world, to take up space, and she got busy making the world a better place in her own way. It's all in how you look at it. It's all in your mindset.

While we will never be able to control the circumstances and storms of our lives, we do get to choose our responses and the stories we tell ourselves about those experiences. Additionally, we get to choose how we will "show up" in our lives as a result of those empowering stories. How about you?

What was it like in your family of origin? Were there things that were difficult? Things that still make you feel stuck? What stories have you been telling yourself about those experiences? Have you chosen to let it entrap you or empower you to do good in the world? How have you chosen to show up in your life as a result? Would you like to flip the script on those stories and start telling yourself a new story about those experiences? Are you ready to start living a better version of yourself and a better version of your life? You can't change the past, but you can decide that enough is enough and you can stand up for yourself. The choice is yours.

If you are ready to flip the script, I'm going to ask you to take a journey with me. On this journey, imagine that you are a building inspector looking at the condition of the foundation and structure that is supporting the shape of your life. You'll be looking for cracks, misalignment, and damage as clues along the way. Without judgment, I'd like to invite you to observe and notice the memories or feelings that may accompany those observations. Finally, I want to encourage you to keep it all in perspective. Keep coming back to the present, reminding yourself that all you are observing was in the past and that a brighter future awaits.

For me, there are three main events that caused misalignment in the foundation years of my life: my birth father's untimely death at such a young age, my mother's unanticipated mental illness, and my stepfather's emotional withdrawal when my mom lost her baby. How about you? What immediately jumps to your mind when you think of any major events that may have affected the foundation of your life? Can you narrow it down to one or more experiences that may still affect you today?

In the same way that the foundational years of our lives with our family of origin can be misaligned, causing emotional or mental pain, our physical bodies can also become misaligned over time due to improper mechanics, overuse, injury or neglect. Sometimes, physical imbalances can also stem from our minds. It's all connected. Those physical misalignments, often due to something as simple as poor posture, or from feeling defeated, or beat down one too many times, can cause physical pain and injury in both our minds and our bodies.

Practicing the basic alignment principles of Mountain Pose will not only help to minimize those aches and pains and help to restore balance to your body, but also help you master just about every other yoga pose in any yoga class. Yes, I did say this one pose will help you master just about every other yoga pose. It is the key to unlocking just about every other yoga pose and to mastering the asanas, or poses, of yoga.

It's all connected. We are one system, not independent parts. We are a delicately balanced ecosystem. Our issues are literally in our tissues and our posture often reflects our emotions. So, let's set up both our minds and our bodies for success on this journey with the Yoga Mindset Formula. We'll start by grounding our feet and establishing a solid foundation beneath us.

The Yoga Mindset Formula, Day 1

MOVE

My first hot yoga instructor in Singapore taught me to keep my big toes touching and my knees locked while standing. Unfortunately, over time, that stance put a lot of pressure on my hips and knees. It was not sustainable. I found that standing with my feet hip width apart and my knees in a barely-perceptible micro-bend was much more comfortable and sustainable. Additionally, I felt grounded and stable. According to Rolf Gates, "How a student stands in mountain is how she stands in life," so let's find that grounded, integrated, and resilient stance in Mountain Pose.

Mountain Pose Alignment #1: Set the Foundation
Set your timer for five minutes and move!

The Feet

1. Stand with your feet about hip width apart and parallel to each other on your mat.
2. Check to make sure that the 2nd and 3rd toes are approximately in line with the heels.
3. Press the big toes, little toes, right and left edges of both heels into the ground.

The Legs

1. With feet grounded firmly, move the shins forward slightly, bending the knee.

2. Now, contract or activate the calf and thigh muscles to straighten the legs up, but keep that knee-saving micro-bend in the knee— no need to lock your knees.

3. Stand tall and feel the stability and strength of your legs and the grounding of your feet.

Breathwork: Keeping your feet and legs firmly rooted in Mountain Pose, let's move our lungs and breathe. Inhale and exhale for five to six slow counts for each breath below. If that makes you feel a bit claustrophobic, start with fewer breaths and try to work your way up to five to six breaths eventually.

1. Breath #1: As you inhale and exhale, visualize yourself as a tree. Imagine your roots shooting deep into the ground and then see yourself supported, and nourished by the earth. Then, imagine yourself growing tall, strong and resilient.

2. Breath #2: As you inhale and exhale, silently say these words to yourself: "I am" and "I have a right to be here."

3. Breath #3: As you take this last breath, grounding down and rising up, silently say these words to yourself, as well: "Life is not happening TO me. Life is happening FOR me."

4. Repeat breaths 1-3 above as many times as possible until this five-minute segment is complete.

When time is up, notice how you feel. Do you feel grounded? Calmer? Stable? Or do you feel nothing different at all? If nothing, that's okay. Day one is just that. Change takes time. Keep moving forward with this empowering movement for the rest of your day. Ground your feet when possible at home, in the grocery store, in a meeting, at school, at work, at your kids' practices, anywhere and everywhere, and stand tall.

Inhale slowly and exhale as you declare, "I am," simply because you exist. Then, inhale and exhale again as you declare, "I have the right to be here." Let these declarations resonate in your heart, soul, and mind all day. Give yourself permission to take up space in your life, your relationships, your career, your connections, your community, and the world today.

MEDITATE

Take a seat, set your timer for five minutes. Write out your responses to questions six and seven below. If time permits, come back later and answer questions one through five, as well.

1. Who raised you?
2. Did you feel that the basic needs to be seen, heard, loved, supported, and protected in your family were met? Why or why not?
3. Do you know anything about your parents' or guardians' family of origin that may help explain why those basic needs were or were not met?
4. If those needs were not met, how did/does that play out in your life?
5. Are those patterns serving you well?
6. Can you think of one to three experiences from your childhood that you feel are still negatively affecting you today?
7. Can you think of at least one positive result that came from each of those experiences?

MANIFEST

Set your timer for five minutes and start manifesting the life you want. Look for the lessons in the storms of your life, flip the script on any disempowering stories that you may have been telling yourself about them and create new and empowering stories that will help you move forward. Finally, consider how those new stories can help you "show up" in a new way within the relationships of your family of origin!

1. For each negative experience that you listed above, if on the other side of it now, can you list at least one positive result?
    Example:
    Negative Experience - Verbally Abusive Parent/Low Self-Esteem
    Positive Result – Positive Verbal Parenting/Verbally Building Child's Self Esteem

If you can't see any positives right now, that is okay. Take as much time as you need and come back later to finish this section. Go at your own pace.

If you were able to see some positive results or life lessons that can make you better, take a moment to consider the ways that the experience that was meant to harm you actually fueled you towards growth personally, professionally, or in some other way. Consider how it worked FOR you. Consider also how that shift in your thinking could affect how you will "show up" differently for your family of origin moving forward?

Keep in mind that "showing up" doesn't necessarily mean "in person." It could be from a distance, if the situation is unsafe for you or anyone else. In either case, set a specific intention for "showing up" for someone in your family of origin, group, or tribe, today and take action. It could be something as simple as a smile, a prayer, dedicating your practice to someone, a text, or a phone call for starters. Write down your intention in your journal, set a day/time goal for when you plan to take action, and then check it off, or adjust your target date/time, when completed.

PRACTICE

The Yoga Mindset Formula in REAL TIME

Today, or anytime moving forward, before stepping into a difficult family situation, or whenever you find yourself rehearsing any old disempowering or negative stories about your childhood experiences, practice the Yoga Mindset Formula in real time!

1. **MOVE:** Inhale for five to six slow counts and exhale for five to six slow counts, and stand with your feet firmly rooted in Mountain Pose.
2. **MEDITATE:** Say quietly to yourself "Life is not happening *to* me, life is happening *for* me." Remind yourself of the new and empowering stories that you choose to tell yourself about your childhood and then let yourself feel that new reality.
3. **MANIFEST:** Visualize yourself firmly rooted into the ground, supported and nurtured, and then act on your intention to "show up" in a new way within your family, group, or tribe, if safe for all involved. If not safe, consider how you can show up from a distance. Write it down and take action. Be the positive change that you hope to see in your family of origin by your thoughts, your words, and/or your actions today.

The Yoga Mindset Principle #1
I am and I have the right to be here.
The Yoga Mindset Mantra:
Life is not happening *to* me, life is happening *for* me.

Change your mindset, change your life!

CHAPTER 2

I Feel

"I crave your mouth, your voice, your hair/
Silent and starving, I prowl through the streets/
Bread does not nourish me, dawn disrupts me/
All day I hunt for the liquid measure of your steps."

Pablo Neruda, *Love Sonnet XI*

I attended high school in Houston, Texas, in the early 80s, and back then, it was kind of a big deal to have things and a boyfriend. Not understanding who I really was yet, and lacking much parental presence or guidance on that topic, I totally succumbed to that social pressure and drifted in and out of relationships to define myself, my worth and my tribe. Looking back, I wish I had been more confident and able to stand on my own two feet, but you just don't know what you don't know until you know, you know?

I didn't know those things because so much of the focus of our lives was on our mom who was still working through her own mental health issues, the pressure my Dad was constantly under as he was working long hard hours to establish himself in the business world, and their marriage, routinely struggling under the pressure of it all. With all their own personal and marital issues, they just didn't seem to have much extra bandwidth to breathe confidence into me or my sister. Our financial and material needs were well provided for, and I am grateful, but we were still very much on our own otherwise. Summers were different, though.

As soon as school was done during my middle and high school years, my parents would fly me, and my sister, back to Maryland to stay with my wise and crazy fun, Aunt Sharon. She was my mom's youngest sister, and she was ten years older than me. So, when I was thirteen, and she was twenty-three, can you imagine the fun we had together? Summers in Maryland were therapeutic for me. It was like CPR for my life.

In addition to CPR, summers were also a family reunion. Sharon inherited all the cousins during the summer, and she was the alpha of the pack. A child of the 70s, she stood firmly on her own two feet, passionately declaring that she didn't need a man to define her and that she would do life her own way and on her own terms. This resonated so deeply with me. She was a den mother to all of us and still is to this day.

As a free spirit, she gave us a lot of room to just be kids. How my sister and I just needed to be. We ran wild during the summers, and we loved every minute of it. I don't remember wearing shoes for weeks at a time, by choice, but amazingly, my feet were never sore. We were outside from sunup to sundown, running all over the neighborhood completely unsupervised and getting into all sorts of situations we had no business getting into at such young ages, but I never remember feeling unsafe. It was a bit like *The Lord of the Flies,* during the day, with the oldest cousins being the ones in charge and leading all kinds of adventures. At night, we'd go to drive-in movies, or we'd ride the waves of my other crazy Aunt's waterbed while talking to complete strangers on a CB radio. We fell asleep whenever, and wherever, in the house.

Mornings began with cornflakes cereal doused with spoonfuls of sugar and hours of cartoons and shows like *Bugs Bunny, The Jetsons, The Flintstones, Tom and Jerry, Leave it to Beaver, My Three Sons, Bewitched,* and *I Dream of Jeannie.* Lunch was usually something like SpaghettiOs or a bologna with mayonnaise sandwich. Dinner was always 'optional.'

Being so far from all the challenges of our family in Texas, where we walked on eggshells, life was simple and fun, and I felt like I could breathe again. With Sharon, I knew I was seen, heard, and valued. I felt safe. I was cared for, and I was loved despite being a very small and broken thing. Summers in Maryland were healing on so many levels.

She spoke love, acceptance, and confidence into my spirit and taught me to always stand tall, roll my shoulders back and move forward with my goals. I never wanted those summers to end, but it always did, and always too soon. I felt like two different people every year, and I much preferred the summer version of myself.

Back home in Texas, the afterglow would linger for about a day or two, but then it was gone. I'd see that my parents were still struggling individually, and as a married couple, and a sadness would creep back into my heart.

Occasionally, my mom would have a good day, where she was fully present, and when that happened, we'd catch up. She'd ask if I'd been keeping up with my school work and for details on my life in high school, including friends, drill team, and, of course, boys. In between her bi-polar manic lows and highs, she was occasionally just herself and a mom. Some of her best relationship advice, during those rare moments, was to "wait" for the one you truly loved, and I took those words to heart.

I dated several boys during my teen years, but remembering my mom's advice, I always drew the line at their predictable and eventual requests for more. Some called me prude, but I didn't care. It was the one thing that I asserted about my body. As a result of my line in the sand, all of the guys I dated eventually lost interest, and we'd both move on to the next dating relationship.

Around my seventeenth birthday, however, things changed. I was a senior in high school and had just received my acceptance letter to North Texas State University. All the college assessment tests suggested I should be a psychologist, and that seemed interesting to me, so I declared my major as psychology. I was excited at the thought of spreading my wings to fly.

It was spring break, and graduation was just a couple of months away. With college on the horizon, my friends and I were out celebrating the freedom that was so close we could almost taste it. We were cruising Westheimer on a Friday night, heading to the disco and dancing in the car to our favorite songs. It was just my best friends, Tonya and Ivonne and me, and we were having a blast!

We pulled up to a stoplight, and my friend, Ivonne, in the front passenger seat, noticed a handsome guy driving a black BMW to our right. She rolled down the passenger window and started a flirtatious conversation with him. I peeked around her from the middle of the front seat to take a closer look. When I saw him, our eyes locked, my pulse quickened, and I felt extraordinarily warm. I sat back to recover, and the light turned green. Tonya was driving, and she floored it, laughing all the way to the next stoplight.

At the next red light, he pulled up to the side of our car again. This time he asked Ivonne if he could get the name and number of the girl in the middle of the front seat. "Me?" I whispered to myself. Getting even warmer, I was speechless and leaned forward again, looked at him, and smiled. The light turned green, and again Tonya floored it, laughing even louder.

At the third light, he asked again, and I actually gave it to him on a torn piece of paper – a complete stranger. I was out of my mind. I was not the kind of girl that would talk to random men. Well, I was, kind of, but only on a CB radio, back in the day. His name was Jake, and he called me the very next day for a lunch date.

As I walked towards the entrance of the restaurant, I saw him there waiting for me. Tall, dark and handsome, I noticed that both of our smiles grew wider, and our cheeks flushed brighter as we got closer to each other. He commented on how happy he was to see me again and on how I looked and then he opened the door for me. None of my boyfriends had ever been so polite or polished.

In the course of our meal, I found out that he was the son of a wealthy computer software developer who lived in a mansion in Sugarland. It was the kind of neighborhood where the Houston Rockets practiced in their Sports Complex.

I also learned that he was home for spring break from college, where he had almost completed his first year of pre-med. We were both nervous and clearly attracted to each other. Normally, I played along with most guys putting their best foot forward, but this guy was different. I didn't feel like I had as much control of myself or the situation. I felt magnetized to him, but I was trying my hardest to keep myself on my side of the table during our lunch date. Was he 'the one?' I wondered to myself.

We couldn't stay away from each other after that first date. We were together on the phone daily, or in person, for that whole week of spring break. It was like we moved into each other's heads, and we were all that we could think about. I was obsessed, focused, and craving him every single moment of the day. Even when he was gone, we were still connected by phone or his weekend visits back to Houston. I was knee-deep in it and enjoyed every single maddening moment. I felt completely out of control. It was both exhilarating and exhausting.

Mandy Len Catron perfectly summarized romantic relationships in her Ted Talk at TedXChapman U when she asked (paraphrased), "Why do we fall in love? We fall in love because we want a guarantee that someone will love us long term. What we want from love is to be known, to be seen, to be understood. To know and be known. Falling in love feels wonderful, but falling in love and staying in love is not the same thing. Falling in love is the easy part. It's also terrifying, as falling in love is realizing that the other person may or may not love you back. It's admitting that you have a lot to lose. The risks are high, but the rewards are even higher. So, how do you decide who to love? How do you decide to stay in a relationship with someone when it gets difficult? How do you know when to cut and run? The reality is that love doesn't happen to people. People fall in love and stay in love because they make a choice to be."

I chose to be in that all-consuming relationship, knowing full well that my friends were not at all happy about the amount of time I was always "with Jake." At first, they were excited for me. Then they tolerated me. Then they flat out let me know that they were tired of hearing about Jake all the time, but it was too late. I was too far gone. I told them that I was truly sorry, and I was, but I was so caught up in the gravitational pull of his orbit that I wasn't even sure I could free myself if I tried. I tried to help them understand how he was different from any other relationship and that I thought he might be 'the one.' They tried to understand, but they also tried to tell me that it was all a bit too much. I didn't listen. I just figured they didn't understand.

Eventually, he asked me to join him at his college in the fall. It was way past the deadlines for application, but I wanted to give it a try. I quickly dropped all of my hard-earned college plans, applied, and got in at the last second with a declaration of pre-med. Never mind that science and math were not my strong points. I was elated at the thought of our future together as doctors and our shared mission to help others around the world.

We were in "love," and by the end of April, we began planning our mutual medical careers and dreaming together about where it all might lead. I told myself that he was "the one," and I asked if he would be my date for the Senior Prom in May.

We were young, in love, and enjoying each other in every way. I felt like I was living in a dream until the day that I walked in on him in bed with another woman just two weeks into our first month at college.

Time stood still. I froze and slowly inhaled as our eyes locked just above the sheet on his bed. This time there were no smiles or sensations of warmth. There was just the cold realization that I had been so blind. In that soul-crushing moment, I grounded my feet, stood tall, rolled my shoulders back and moved forward. Having lived through years of my parents' struggling marriage, I knew that I wanted none of it and that there was no future for us. I expected more and I wanted better for myself. I exhaled, turned, and left without ever looking back.

In a Ted Talk by Katie Hood, she wondered aloud, "Isn't it interesting that we've never actually been taught how to love? The truth is that we often harm and disrespect the ones we love. In the course of our life, 100% of us will be on the receiving end of unhealthy behaviors, and 100% of us will do unhealthy things. It's part of being human. In its worst form, the harm we inflict on others shows up as abuse and violence. The truth is that unhealthy relationships are all around us. Pay attention to how your relationship grows." Great advice. If only I had known it back then.

Jake tried to reach me by phone and through friends, but I wasn't interested. I wanted nothing to do with him. I ignored all the red flags and didn't want to continue being the fool in the relationship. Unfortunately, we still had a lot of classes together.

In those classes, he routinely sat right next to me and would slip me notes trying to communicate, but I couldn't do it. I would start shaking in a complete rage that brought me to the edge of tears every time. I was so easily overcome by the emotions of what I thought was love now mixed with hate and self-loathing. Seeing him just made me feel terrible about not seeing the red flags, not listening to my friends, and not going with my gut sooner.

Intellectually, I had decided we were done, but emotionally, I still had intense feelings for him. I couldn't snap my fingers and turn off those feelings despite his actions. It would take time for the feelings to subside, and the hands on the clock couldn't go fast enough for me.

I tried to avoid him in classes, but he kept sitting next to me. When that happened, I simply got up and walked out of class. Not the smartest move when you need to listen to a lecture, but it was either that or publicly dissolve into a puddle of tears. Shaking uncontrollably, I usually kept it together until I was out of the classroom, but then I couldn't stop the tears. Crazy, I know, but when you are eighteen, from a strict and sheltered family, you are not too wise to the ways of the world. I wasn't cynical or clever or confident enough yet to know how to tell him to get lost and just casually move on with my life. I just knew that I didn't want him to see that he could still affect me so profoundly. I didn't want him to see that he still had access to so much of my heart.

Disillusioned, wounded, and struggling, I needed help. I wanted to talk to my parents, but they were still knee deep in their own struggles. I wanted to talk to my friends, but they had all let me know that they had heard quite enough of Jake. Feeling like those were my only options, I internalized the suffocating weight of all of it instead.

I didn't know where or how to begin to recover the balance. I actually even remember asking myself at one point if it, if I, was even worth the effort. I honestly wasn't sure for a while, and that was a terrifying place to be.

I tried to numb the pain and fill the hole in my heart with clubbing, parties, and all kinds of "recreational" activities. Every morning, I'd wake up a little worse than the day before. My sweet Southern Baptist roommate watching my slow, painful and downward spiral, always let me know that she was praying for me and that she was there if I ever wanted to talk. I usually laughed at the thought of her praying for me because I felt like I was way beyond the reach of God. I was sure that He'd given up on me, so I'd pretty much given up on Him. I'd also given up on school. I attended classes only periodically because it was too difficult to see Jake. I couldn't focus when he was in the same room, and my grades started to reflect the struggle.

When I started failing all of my classes, I eventually gave up on everything, including myself. I chopped off my hair, stopped caring about my appearance, and started writing dark poetry. I couldn't see a way forward.

They say that what you project is what you attract. Well, I am living proof that this is true. In that state of mind, I seemed to be attracting people just like me: the lost, the outsiders, the confused, and the misunderstood. I managed quite a while in this state of being with my new 'friends', without any serious issues, but one night, it all caught up with me.

Returning to the dorms, after another inglorious night of 'recreational escapism,' I was not well. My heart rate accelerated, making it hard to breathe normally. I felt hot, thirsty, and sick to my stomach. Sweating profusely and stumbling from one wall to another in my dorm hallway, I saw some of the holier-than-thou Christian girls on my floor quietly giggling and whispering about me. No doubt, I was the talk of the hall, but anyone could tell that something was very wrong with me that night. I was in distress, and yet none of those girls asked if I was okay or if I needed help. "Hypocrites," I thought to myself. If that was Christianity at a Christian college, I didn't want any part of it.

I somehow made it to my room, burst through the door, and collapsed on my bed. My roommate, Lori, sweet Christian Lori, was by my side immediately, asking what happened, if I was okay, and if she could do anything. She was the one and only true Christian that I knew on the floor. Realizing that things were a bit more serious than normal, she took action as I was fading in and out. She helped me undress, gave me some water, and cared for me until I fell asleep. I wasn't walking with God at that point in my life, but her kindness was like God's perfect love in real time that night.

That next morning, when I woke up, I was shocked to be alive. Barely able to talk, I was parched. After several glasses of water, I thanked Lori for helping me and apologized for being the worst roommate ever. She brushed away my comments with a wave of her hand and instead invited me to join her on her drive home for the weekend.

Feeling wiped out and ashamed of myself, I thanked her, but politely declined, saying that I probably wasn't in the best shape for travel or for visiting with anyone's parents. Again, she brushed away my protests and told me that I didn't have to be social and that I could just rest and recover in the privacy of her bedroom. She asked again and added the words, "please," and, "for me?" I could see she was determined, and I certainly owed her, so I said, "sure, why not?" That was my answer to everyone and everything those days.

I remember getting into her car that Saturday morning, but I don't remember much of the ride. I was in and out of lucidity after God only knows what was in my body the night before. I really only remember arriving at her house, meeting her parents briefly, and then sleeping the rest of the day away in her bed. The family just let me be. How I just needed to be.

I woke up and noticed it was pitch dark outside. Had I slept the whole day? I was disoriented, but the smell of food pulled me down the stairs and towards the kitchen. It was nighttime, and Lori's mom was cooking dinner. I was still parched and now also starving. Lori and her Dad were sitting at the table talking with each other.

Without missing a step, as I walked closer to the table, her dad took the lead and invited me to join them. The meal was delicious, and thankfully, they didn't overwhelm me with too many questions. Mostly they just inquired as to whether or not I was comfortable or if I needed anything. Their sensitivity and discretion were so appreciated, and I could see that their hospitality and concern was genuine. Now I understood where Lori's kindness originated. I figured that Lori had brought them up to speed on everything that had happened in our dorm room over the months and especially the night before we arrived.

The final comment from her parents was an invitation to join them for church the next morning before going back to school. I really didn't want to go, but after allowing me to stay at their house, sleep in their daughter's bed all day and eat their food, I felt more than obligated. So, I said, "sure, why not?"

Church was the absolute last place on earth that I wanted to be that Sunday morning. Having been raised Catholic, but no longer practicing, a hefty dose of good Catholic guilt made a return visit to my nervous system. I had been taught in the Catholic Church that God was so holy, and I was so *not* holy and so *not* worthy to be in His presence. The Catholic nuns drilled that into me at school, and where they left off, the Priests at every Mass kept the narrative going. I surely would not be worthy in my current state, but it was too late to get out of it now.

On our way to church, I was once again watching the dashed lines of the road whisk by while thinking, "How in the world did it come to this?" The exact same thoughts I had when my mom was rushed to the ER after she attempted suicide, but this time it was me who was dying inside and in need of life support.

I don't remember much about the church, but I do remember that it was not a Catholic church. Lori and her family attended a nondenominational Christian church and it was very different. I felt like the preacher was speaking right to me the whole time, not in words of fire and brimstone, but in gentle whispers of love and compassion. That was new to me in a church setting. It felt as if he knew exactly what was going on inside of me and knew exactly what I needed to hear. He talked about the story of the Prodigal Son and of how life happens, and about how we all tend to stray from ourselves and God, but then he reminded us that God never strays from us. He spoke of God as a good and loving Father who never leaves us and always stands with open arms, ready to receive us when we choose to turn to Him. I felt so overwhelmed by this concept of God as my good and loving Father and the concept of God's grace and love for the Prodigal Child.

When the preacher gave the altar call towards the end of the service, something crazy came over me. I didn't even know what an altar call was at that time. I was a lapsed Catholic, for heaven's sakes! I just knew that I needed some divine love, grace and healing in my life. As a properly guilt-ridden Catholic and a complete introvert, I would never, ever, *ever*, have responded to an altar call. It would have drawn far too much attention to myself, but that morning, I felt compelled by something much bigger than myself. I felt like I heard the whisper of the Spirit of God inviting me to rest and empowering me to walk. I remember getting up and walking forward immediately after the call was given, without a second thought, and then noticing that Lori was right beside me, again supporting me in love and presence. Feeling the flood of emotion rise as I got closer to the altar, the release was profound. That step, that decision, to move forward in faith, towards a God of grace, compassion and healing, towards the Creator of everything, was the first step in helping me find my way back home. It was the beginning of a meaningful relationship with the Creator and a significant step away from religion.

That was the first of many turning points in my life where I realized that I didn't have to be the victim of my circumstances any longer. I learned that I could flip the script in my life. I could choose to learn the lessons in the challenges. Nothing about my situation had changed. I was still failing all my classes. I'd still neglected myself horribly. Jake was still there. My heart was still crushed. The emotions were still there, but something about me was different. I had reconnected with the Creator of everything. In the process, I had started to remember who I was and that I was of inestimable value in myself. I decided to receive the love of God, and I decided to love myself again. I also started to see that, indeed, it, life, and I, was worth it. I was able to see the worth in Jake, too. I realized that he was human and imperfect, just like me and everyone else in the world, and I was finally able to forgive him. Most importantly, I was finally able to forgive myself. I was finally free and realized that I was hating the wrong things, myself and Jake, all along.

According to Dr. Henry Cloud, there are 'deja vu' people in the world who have experienced abusive relationships and won't tolerate it a second time. He said they hate wisely and he invites everyone else to do the same. He wrote that in relationships, "just as water seeks the lowest level, dysfunction seeks the lowest level of tolerance. If your standard for what you require in life and in relationships is low, bad things will ooze into your life, just as water dribbles to the lowest spot of ground. If you allow mistreatment, then people who mistreat others will find you, and you will get what you tolerate. However, deja vu people, you will notice, simply do not tolerate dysfunction. They hate it - wisely. They send out the antibodies, mark it for what it is, and end it. They do not destroy the person or the relationship in the process, but they do not tolerate the infection. So, choosing what you hate is serious business."

Though my life still felt like a hot mess, I started telling myself a new story. I told myself that had I not had the experience of seeing a challenging marriage with my parents, I may have tolerated Jake's behavior and gone on with the relationship. Who knows! I may have even gone on to marry Jake and been living in hell while he fooled around in one affair after another. I told myself that what felt like life happening to me during my middle and teen years, was actually happening for me, for precisely the moment I found Jake in bed with another woman.

Once I was also able to flip the script on that soul-crushing moment in my life, I was filled with gratitude for the lessons of the struggle. I was also able to see that had that betrayal never happened, the path to my husband today, my best friend and soulmate, would never have happened. I actually thank God for that soul-crushing betrayal as it led me to the best possible marriage. I would have missed the miracle otherwise. It was exactly what was needed to get me to where I am and wanted to be today. It's completely counterintuitive to flow with the storms of life, but if you trust that everything is always happening for you, you will be able to move forward towards your best life quicker.

In the same way that I recovered that balance in my mind, I had to get my physical body back in order, too. I had to start caring for myself again with my diet, exercise and general self-care. Sometimes our bodies get out of alignment for a variety of reasons, and they need to be realigned in order to move forward, as well. So let's shift gears and pick up where we left off with our physical body.

In the last chapter, we discussed the importance of setting the foundation and grounding the feet—the foundation of our body and our lives. In this chapter, we'll move up from the feet and the legs to the hips. This part of our body relates to our creativity, our reproductive organs and our intimate relationships. The goal of alignment in this part of our body is to find and maintain that "sweet spot" between pushing the hips too far back or pulling the hips too far forward.

Think about your hips and their role in your daily life for a moment. It's common knowledge that most people sit more than stand every day. When people sit for the majority of the day, the hips are mostly bent or contracted and tight.

That contracted position leads to a very common condition called lower cross syndrome, which is just a fancy way of saying that most people have tight hip flexors from sitting so much and weak lower back muscles, causing a lot of lower back pain and a hunched forward stance. Sound familiar? If so, good news, Mountain Pose can help.

The Yoga Mindset Formula, Day 2

MOVE

Mountain Pose Alignment Principle #2: Find Neutral
Set your timer for five minutes and move!

The Pelvis

1. Stand with your feet about hip width apart, ensure that the second and third toes are in line with heels and that the four corners of your feet (big toes, little toes, and both sides of the heels) are pressing down firmly on the ground, causing your arches to elevate slightly. Your shins are forward slightly, and your thighs are activated and pulled back, and you are standing tall. The feet and legs are strong, and there is a barely perceptible micro bend in the knee.

2. Shift your hips, also referred to as the pelvis, too far back and then shift your hips too far forward. Yes, we are going to the extremes. Next, bring your pelvis to a neutral position between the two extremes by tucking the tailbone down towards the floor slightly, but maintain that natural S-curve of the lower spine.

3. Contract the abdominal muscles tightly below the belly button, pull the rib cage back slightly and then stand tall by lifting your heart.

Scan your body. How does this neutral hip position feel? It may be a bit strange, if your hips have been to one extreme or the other for years, but this is how we were meant to stand: with our pelvis in neutral, maintaining that gentle S curve of the lower back with our feet grounded, our legs strong, and our hearts lifted to the world.

Expanding those alignment principles to our intimate relationships, ask yourself if you currently lean a bit too far to the side of extreme emotion or too far to the opposite side of too little emotion? Consider the changes that would be needed to bring those relationships to a more neutral, balanced, and healthy state of being. Is that something you want? Do you believe that you are meant to relate to others in grounded, strong, balanced, and healthy relationships?

Breathwork: Inhale slowly for five to six counts and exhale slowly for five to six counts for each breath below.

1. Visualize yourself as a majestic tree. Imagine your roots shooting deep and wide into the ground beneath you. Then, see yourself firmly rooted, connected, supported, nurtured, growing tall, strong, resilient, and flowing in the wind.
2. As you visualize yourself also firmly grounded into the earth, flowing light and airy above, quietly say to yourself, "I am," and, "I have a right to be here."
3. Coming back to your physical body, see your hips perfectly balanced, with the tailbone tucked down slightly towards the earth, and quietly say to yourself, "I feel," and, "I have the right to feel both emotionally and physically in healthy and balanced relationships."
4. Finally, standing grounded, strong, and balanced, quietly say to yourself, "Life is not happening to me. Life is happening for me."

When done, take these thoughts with you and apply those subtle adjustments to your pelvis and your relationships. At first, the changes might not be noticeable, but over time you may start to perceive the benefits in reduced back pain, increased core strength, and increased flexibility. Standing in a grounded, strong, and balanced way also conveys something about yourself to the world. It speaks of confidence. If that is something you want to project, start with the feet and hips every day.

Consider the health of your current relationships with your friends, co-workers or your significant other. According to motivational speaker and author, Mel Robbins, "All relationships are based on the desire for either control or connection." If someone in a relationship is seeking connection, they will find ways to acknowledge, celebrate and support you. If, on the other hand, someone in a relationship is seeking power, they will find ways to control, criticize and dominate you.

If you find yourself in a controlling relationship, it's vitally important to remember that you are not usually the issue. The issue usually lies with the controlling person, who is more than likely driven by fear. In these situations, and only if it's safe for you and everyone else involved, you will need to find your voice to teach that person how to treat you. They simply won't know your boundaries until you define them clearly. Easy to say, but hard to do for a lot of people. We'll go into more detail on finding and using your voice in Chapter 5. In the meantime, let's meditate on the concept of healthy and balanced relationships.

MEDITATE

Take a seat, set your timer for five minutes. Answer questions seven and eight below. Come back later as time permits to answer the other questions.

1. Do you tend towards controlling or connecting in your relationships? Why, or why not?
2. Do you feel like you are in a controlling relationship now? If so, which one/ones?
3. Do you have any insight into why the other person might be so controlling?
4. Have you clearly defined your boundaries in the relationships? If not, why not?
5. Are there people who are trying to connect with you in a relationship? Who? Why?
6. Are you resisting or welcoming those efforts at connection? Why or why not?
7. Can you think of some experiences you've had in romantic relationships that you feel are still negatively affecting you today?
8. Can you think of at least one or more positive results that came from each of those experiences?

MANIFEST

Set your timer for five minutes and manifest your life! See how life is happening for you, then flip the script on your experiences and decide how you will "show up" differently within your intimate relationships!

1. Write the name of a person with whom you were, or are, in an intimate relationship.
2. Think about the state of that relationship. Was/Is it healthy, unhealthy, balanced, unbalanced, supportive, challenging, toxic, or satisfying? Create or pick a word and put it next to that person's name.
3. You will never be able to change or control the other person, but you can flip the script for yourself in those relationships and choose to see the positive in a negative experience. If possible, write out at least one positive that came from a negative experience with that person, and then with that new story in mind, choose how you would like to "show up" differently moving forward as a result of that lesson learned. Set your intention by putting a word next to that person's name describing how you plan to show up differently and then take action in person, if safe, or from a distance, if not safe.

Let's put this all into practice in real time with the Yoga Mindset!

PRACTICE

The Yoga Mindset in REAL TIME

Today, or anytime, when you wish to improve your intimate relationships outside of your family of origin, apply the Yoga Mindset in real time!

1. **MOVE:** Inhale slowly for five to six counts and exhale slowly for five to six counts. Stand in Mountain Pose with your pelvis in a neutral position.
2. **MEDITATE:** Declare quietly to yourself, "Life is not happening *to* me, life is happening *for* me."
3. **MANIFEST:** Visualize yourself in healthy and balanced relationships and then act on your intention to flip the script on the disempowering stories you may have been telling yourself. Use the power of that new story to find a new way to "show up" in your relationships, beyond your family of origin. Let yourself feel what balanced and healthy relationships would look, sound and feel like in your life.

The Yoga Mindset Principle #2:
I have the right to feel both emotionally and physically.
The Yoga Mindset Mantra:
Life is not happening *to* me, life is happening *for* me.

Change your mindset, change your life!

CHAPTER 3

I Do

"Our deepest fear is not that we are inadequate.
Our deepest fear is that we are powerful beyond measure.
It is our light, not our darkness, that most frightens us.
We ask ourselves, 'Who am I to be brilliant, gorgeous, talented, fabulous?'
Actually, who are you not to be?"

Marianne Williamson

After my literal come to Jesus moment, things were very different for me when I returned to college. Nothing about my circumstances had changed, but I had. I was grounded again, and I had decided that it, life, and I, was worth it. I was able to see that there was nothing left for me at the college, and so I set some new goals and decided to start moving in a new direction.

I quickly dropped all of my classes, resigned and moved to Charlottesville, Virginia, where my stepfather's job had transferred him at the end of my senior year in High School. Though it was hard to leave all that was familiar, the move gave me a clean slate and a new place to begin again.

It was December of 1984 in Charlottesville, Virginia. Naked trees punctuated the gently rolling hills covered in thick layers of snow. It was quite a change from the flat terrain and year-round warm temps of Texas. I remember thinking that the winter scenery was such a reflection of my life from the outside looking in. I'd failed most of my classes, I didn't look anything like myself, and my spirit was still wounded. You couldn't tell from the outside, but change and growth were occurring deep within. It was small, quiet, and hidden, but it was happening, and spring would be coming soon. U2, Yaz, and Tears for Fears were my constant companions as I licked my wounds and healed.

I found a new church that was stale with tradition, picked up a new waitressing job at Chi-Chi's, and enrolled at the local community college to salvage what I could of my first college semester GPA. I dated a few guys on the rebound, still desiring a relationship, but I was not exactly fully present. It was more like going through the motions or practicing dating again. I was still healing.

That spring, when I felt about fifty percent healed, I dared to dream a little bigger. I applied to Virginia Tech and was quickly accepted. I wanted to study art, but my stepfather drew a deep line in the sand saying, "No. I'm not going to have a starving artist living in my basement forever." He told me to get a real degree that would lead to a real job that would pay the bills instead. I died a little when he said that, but since he was paying the bills, I felt I had no choice and declared myself as a Business Major.

As a creative spirit, I did not do very well in business. When not studying, I worked as a waitress at a swanky piano bar called The Cuckoo's Nest to help pay for my car insurance and to distract me from mind-numbing accounting classes.

Quite a few Architecture students were working at the Cuckoo's Nest, and I hung on every word about their lives in the Architecture School and their various design projects. Architecture seemed to be both the art that would satisfy my need to create and the science that would satisfy my stepfather's need to pay the bills. So, I made the decision to change my major and apply. The only thing holding me back from my new goal was buy-in from my parents. My Dad seemed hesitant, but my mom, now more stabilized on medication, told me that she thought it was a great idea and that I could do anything I set my mind to doing. She told me that she'd talk with Dad and get back to me about it soon. Eventually, I received their blessing.

I applied to the School of Architecture and was admitted to their intensive first-year design studio summer program. I loved every brain-altering minute. Additionally, I felt like I had finally found my tribe. We were contemplative, empathetic, mostly introverted but highly opinionated, intellectually curious, creative dreamers, designers, and thinkers who found meaning and magic in everything.

Several of us took poetry and astronomy classes for design inspiration and felt called to become vegetarians in order to save the world. I remember wearing my "Save the Cows" t-shirt to a poetry class and wondering why one non-architecture student was even asking why I wanted to save the Holsteins. In utter farming ignorance, I rolled my eyes and refused to answer him.

Now, older, wiser, and married to a man that raised cows when he was younger, I realize how silly I must have sounded. At the same time, that was par for the course for architectural design students. We were all marching to the beat of a completely different drummer.

The calculated placement of every floor, wall, window, and soaring roofline of our fledgling architectural projects were positively sacred and profoundly important. We were determined to make the world a better place, one well-designed building at a time.

I was in the process of recovering my balance, forgetting Jake, rebuilding my self-confidence, and reconnecting with the core of who I was that summer. I was about eighty percent healed during the summer intensive, and I was feeling a lightness in my spirit again. In addition to connecting to the core of who I was, I also reconnected with my physical core when I started to take some exercise classes on the campus. It was a bit of a shock to the system, but a good one.

For most people, the core, which is everything but arms, legs, and head, is one of the most utilized and one of the most neglected parts of the body. We use our core to lift, carry, haul, reach, push, pull, and twist through our lives daily. We assume it will just keep functioning, often without any focused strengthening or flexibility exercises, and then we wonder why it hurts or is injured so easily.

Core strength is absolutely critical for total health and wellness. In my experience as a fitness instructor and personal trainer, most clients tell me that they want to lose weight, sculpt their arms, hips, thighs and, especially, tone and tighten their abs. They usually ask if I can help them get a 'six-pack' quickly. I always tell them that a 'six-pack' can definitely be the result of a strong core and then explain what that actually means. The core is so much more than a 'six-pack.' The core is everything except your neck, head, arms, hands, legs, and feet. It's the abs, sides *and* the back.

Everyone loves a good bench press, an impressive pushup, or washboard abs, but not too many people go to the gym pumped to sculpt their rhomboids or their erector spinae. The result? People in gyms are often hunched over with tight chests and abdominal muscles, while their upper and lower back muscles are stretched and weak. There is an imbalance in the core, and that is when injuries are more likely to occur around the back area.

Putting on my personal trainer hat, I'd like to propose a different way of thinking about what the core is and how to take care of it. Expand your concept of the core from a two-dimensional six-pack to a three dimensional stabilized, integrated and balanced core. Next, try the Yoga Mindset Formula to keep the core strong. It is the perfect workout to strengthen all the core muscles: the front, back and the sides.

Most of my clients tell me that they feel like their core is not strong, and for most people, that is true. The good news, however, is that, in most cases, it can be strengthened with some very specific exercises. Alternatively, sometimes a weak core may simply be the result of poor posture. There's a yoga pose for that, too. It's Mountain Pose, and if you practice it consistently, you can strengthen your core, improve your posture and reduce back pain.

Consistency in practicing anything always wins. Intensity is impressive for a moment, but consistency delivers long term and sustainable results. If you are looking to strengthen, tone, and tighten your core, practicing Mountain Pose, in addition to a heart-healthy diet, can help to get you there.

There are so many different diets on the market that it's overwhelming. I generally avoid diets like the plague because they simply don't work. One program, however, made a profound difference in my life, and that was Wildfit because it approached our relationship with food from an evolutionary and seasonal point of view. I'm not a nutritionist, so I can't recommend any diet or nutrition plan, but if interested in finding out more about this approach to food, check it out at www.getwildfit.com, and always seek the advice of a doctor before beginning any new program of nutrition.

While exercising and eating a healthy diet seems like a no-brainer, it actually requires effort and a conscious decision, or intention, to do the work consistently. It's a lifestyle decision to take extraordinary care of yourself physically, mentally, spiritually, and nutritionally. Think about that for a moment. Are there things in your life that you take extraordinary care of? Things like stylish glasses, a retainer, your newest cell phone, cars, fingernails, expensive purses, your new house, or manicured lawns, just to name a few?

Have you ever considered that the degree to which you care for something shows the degree to which you value something? Think about that for a moment, too. What do you take very good care of in your life? How about yourself? Do you value yourself and take care of yourself more than your yard or your car, or any other person or material possession? If taking care of yourself is low on the list of your priorities, consider how you can reprioritize. How can you start to value and better care for yourself? Better diet? More sleep? The Yoga Mindset daily? Minimizing time on social media or computers? You probably know what needs to change. Put another way, if you have an expensive car, purse, or watch, for example, and it becomes damaged, would it really be as critical as your health going by the wayside? Hopefully not!

Hopefully, you are starting to see that it's vitally important to make your health and wellness a top priority so that you can increase your odds of living longer in order to be all that you hope to be and do for yourself and others in this lifetime. Wondering where to begin? Start with your nutrition.

It's so cliche, but in so many ways, you are what you eat. Are you fueling your body with optimum nutrition, including whole, ideally organic, foods, including a wide variety of vegetables and protein daily? Are you staying hydrated with water? Are you sleeping about eight hours a day? Are you making daily movement a priority? Or, are you fueling your body with processed foods, sugar, sodas, alcohol, little sleep, and minimal exercise?

I understand that we are all at different places in our lives. I suspect doctors just get sleep when they can. New moms are definitely trying to get sleep when they can, too. Sometimes it seems like processed food is all a person can afford, too. Still, if the goal is to care for yourself, perhaps a few new goals can help jumpstart the process. For example, instead of soda, could you drink water? It's a small change that can make a big difference to your physical health over the long term. Wherever you are, and whatever positive changes you can implement, make a plan that is best for you and start moving forward.

Do you really believe that you are more important than any material thing in the world? If no one has treated you as someone of great value, or you've never treated yourself as someone of great value, today could be a new beginning for you. It's your choice as to how you will value yourself. If living well for as long as possible is a goal for you, see yourself as valuable and care for yourself as the rare and priceless treasure that you are.

Starting the process of caring for your heart and physically strengthening your body, especially your core, may feel strange if it's been neglected for a while. But eventually, with consistency, you may start to notice improved posture, a reduction in back pain, and a sense of increased physical wellbeing. I had to strengthen both the core of who I was and the physical core of my body when I moved to Virginia. It took time, but eventually, I recovered my balance and was one hundred percent again. Now it's your turn.

In the next segment of the Yoga Mindset Formula, you'll work on sealing your core. To seal your core, imagine a corset or plastic wrap encircling your core. Weird, I know, but just go with it for a visual. Next, imagine someone pulling the strings, or the plastic wrap, tight behind you. You would feel that tightness on the front, back, and sides of your core. Now extend that contraction to your lower abdominal muscles below the navel. Most importantly, without letting the abdominal muscles go, breathe. It's a lot to do all at once, but practice makes progress.

Keep those core muscles tight, lift your heart, and stand tall daily. Think of an imaginary string on the top of your head pulling you up gently towards the ceiling. Think of stacking the vertebrae, one on top of the other, above that beautifully neutral pelvis, and that natural S curved spine. This is a subtle posture adjustment of a few millimeters or inches, but for others, it may feel like a radical shift measured in miles.

Some people may have lived the majority of their life hunched over a desk, a phone, or a computer. In contrast, others may have lived the majority of their lives hunched over, feeling defeated or devastated by one too many hard knocks in life. If you can relate to either of these examples and honestly, these examples apply to most of us at one point or another, take your time with this movement practice. Give yourself permission to lift your heart up one more time, to stand tall again. Feel into it. If it's been a while, just notice how you feel in this empowering stance. Every single day, in every circumstance, sitting or standing, give yourself permission to plant your feet firmly on the ground, to strengthen your legs beneath you, to seal your core, and to lift your heart to the world again. You have the right to be, to feel, to dream, to set goals, and to achieve them one step at a time. Do you believe it? Is your posture reflecting it? This simple act of sealing your core and lifting your heart will help you stand tall and reinforce the mindset that you have the right to set goals and do the work to achieve them.

Now, when you start the practice of standing tall, people may notice something different about you. They might even ask if you've lost some weight. Standing tall is a little secret to help you look thinner, in case you didn't know. Strange, but true. Prepare yourself for the comments of others and just notice how they react. If you feel led to share, feel free to let them know you've started reading *The Yoga Mindset* and that standing tall in Mountain Pose is one the many exercises in the book (shameless plug…).

Not everyone will be onboard with the changes you are making. Most people don't like change. Some may even feel threatened by you standing a little taller and they may see your new way of being as arrogant. Some may try to help you back down to size, as they prefer you to be. If you experience this kind of reaction, it may be a sign of the other person's insecurity. Keep in mind that it is their issue, not yours, and move forward with confidence.

Think of animals in the wild. The alpha usually stands the tallest as the other animals in the pack cower and cringe to show their deference.

In no way am I suggesting that you seek to stand tall just to make others cower. We are not a pack of wolves. We are people and that is the greatest miracle of all. Every single one of us has a right to stand tall for that reason alone.

Remind yourself that you have the right to be present, to feel, to dream, to set goals, to do the work to achieve them and to stand tall in confidence, simply because you are. Any comments to the contrary are one hundred percent the other person's issue. Don Miguel Ruiz confirmed this when he declared in his blessedly thin book, *The Four Agreements*, that "nothing other people do is because of you. It is because of themselves."

You have the right to give yourself permission to change and though it may trigger some people along the way, keep moving forward. Take note of those that seem threatened and those that applaud and encourage the change. Those reactions will tell you a lot about the people in your life. Use that information to decide who to surround yourself with on your journey. To the extent that you can, love those who feel threatened, perhaps from a distance, and seek out those who will support and applaud your efforts at self-improvement in a closer relationship.

Relationships with other people are so interesting. They take a lot of time and effort, don't they? Sometimes personalities blend well, and sometimes they don't. If you are in a relationship where you are trying to stand tall, but feel like you are always under attack, it may not be you at all. It may be that it's not the right relationship fit. Now, don't get me wrong. I'm not suggesting that anyone drop a relationship at the first sign of a challenge. Relationships take time and effort, and in most cases, it's worth the effort. Give a relationship a chance to grow and develop before pushing the eject button. I need to reiterate here that abuse in a relationship is a different thing altogether. In those situations where you are fearful that someone is a danger to themselves, you, or someone else, I strongly recommend seeking professional help. If you are not growing as a person in a relationship, something may need to change.

Dr. Henry Cloud gave us a blueprint for personal development and growth as a person in relationships when he wrote, "look to wise, loving people to help you. Find a support group, a counselor, or a coach. There is no magic formula that tells you where help has to come from. But there is a formula that says if you do not have help, you are not going to get as far. Sometimes outside structure is needed to accomplish things for which you lack the discipline to accomplish alone. Growth is a process. Give up your demand to have it all together right now. Whatever you choose to accomplish, you will get it wrong more than once as you move toward your goal. Failure is part of the process. And no one who got there did it without failing. No one–get used to it. A winner is someone who steps out, fails, regroups, and instead of beating himself up, learns from the mistake and tries again… Banish false beliefs… Identify them by listening to how you talk to yourself. Keep a journal of those negative thoughts. Write down where they come from – what experience in your life painted such pessimism? Then change each negative belief into a positive one that reflects the way you want to believe and can be translated into reality. Learn to talk back to those debilitating beliefs as you hear them come up in your head. Research has shown over and over that as people monitor and challenge those belief systems, their lives change. Put your vision and goals on paper. If you have no plan or goals to get you somewhere, you will end up nowhere. But if you have written out your visions and goals, you are more likely to reach them. Write down the big vision and plan out small but achievable steps that will get you there. Put dates to each step. Review your plan often. Do not see success in love or life as a goal that you cannot attain or a prize only for special or lucky people. That is not true. Success is never embodied in a person but in the ways of wisdom that transcend any one individual."

What's your big plan? What are your big goals for your life? Have you written it down as a plan? Ready to start making the plan, but not sure where to begin? Give yourself space and time to think about it. I suspect that deep in the core of your being, you know what it would look like for you. Surround yourself with people that will support and celebrate your progress. Minimize exposure to those who will hold you back from reaching your goals. Practice the Yoga Mindset Formula to help you get there one breath at a time.

The Yoga Mindset Formula, Day 3

MOVE

Mountain Pose Alignment Principle #3: Seal the Core
Set your timer for five minutes and move!

The Abdominal Muscles:

1. Set your foundation with your feet rooted firmly into the ground, about hip width apart, with the second and third toes in line with the heels, shins forward, thighs back, legs strong, and standing tall. Add that knee-saving micro bend, rock the pelvis forward and back and then find that healthy and balanced neutral position for the pelvis and let's seal the core.

2. Measure about three to four fingers below the belly button. This is the focal point of your contraction. Remember that concept of a corset around your body. Imagine someone starting to pull the strings tight behind you. Not so tight that you can't breathe, but tight enough that you contract on the front, back, and sides of your core. Then, from deep inside, as if you were trying to stop the flow of your urine in the bathroom, contract the muscles of the pelvic floor and then lift your heart to stand tall. Gently maintain this alignment throughout your day, and remember to breathe as you go.

If you can't quite feel any abdominal contractions at this point, we have a different hack for you. Sometimes the pelvic floor and abdominal muscles need a little time and extra help if they haven't been activated in quite a while. In these situations, we use props! Repeat after me: props are my friend.

Every seasoned yoga practitioner knows this to be true as props can help everyone reach much deeper and fuller levels of expression in a yoga pose. Embrace the props. If you have one, grab a yoga block about four inches thick and squeeze it gently between your knees. If you don't have one, a rolled up towel might do the trick.

This squeezing action will help to automatically contract those deeper abdominal and pelvic floor muscles. Easy on the squeeze. If you feel any pain, anywhere, back off immediately. The goal of yoga is not perfection, but progress. Stay in close contact with your body as you move for feedback. Find a way of being with movement that best serves you moment by moment. If you feel pain at any time, adjust. Always feel free to modify any pose in any way as needed for your body.

Prop, or no prop, you might notice that your upper body has hunched forward in the process of sealing the core. Hold on. That is just the body compensating for the slightly tucked pelvis and the contracted abdominal muscles. We'll correct for that hunching motion with the next segment, the ribs and the sides of the body often referred to as "the side bodies" in the yoga world. The term seems odd to me, but now you are in the know.

Ribs & Sides of the Body:

1. Holding the contraction of your core, next start to lift your heart and the sides of your body up (often referred to as the "side bodies" in yoga) while shifting the rib cage back slightly.
2. Stack your spine directly over that neutral pelvis. How does this feel?

3. Hit the boundaries. Hunch forward, then open up tall. Finally, find that balanced, aligned, and neutral position where the core is contracted but not stiff, and the heart is open but not overly relaxed.

Breathwork: Inhale slowly for five to six counts and exhale slowly for five to six counts for each breath below.

Breath 1: Set your foundation and quietly declare to yourself, "I am," and "I have the right to be here."

Breath 2: Bring your pelvis to neutral and quietly declare to yourself, "I feel," and "I have the right to feel, both emotionally and physically."

Breath 3: Seal your core and quietly declare to yourself, "I do," and "I have the right to set goals and accomplish them."

Breath 4: Declare to yourself, "Life is not happening TO me. Life is happening FOR me."

When done, aim to maintain those thoughts and those subtle adjustments to your core throughout your day. At first, the changes might not be noticeable, but over time you will start to perceive the benefits. In the next segment of the Yoga Mindset Formula, to fully enjoy those benefits, I'm going to ask you to be selfish.

If any of this is resonating with you, join me online for a FREE 3 Day Yoga Mindset Challenge where you will see the movement, meditation, and manifestation segments in real-time, in addition to yoga classes and alignment hacks to every yoga pose! Prioritize your health and wellness. You are worth it. Visit this link to sign up:

www.mosaicconcepts.com/yogachallenge

MEDITATE

Take a seat, set your timer for five minutes. Answer questions five and six below. Come back later as time permits to answer the other questions. Learn to see things as they actually are in your life regarding your self-confidence in yourself, in your relationships with others, and in your ability to set and accomplish your personal goals!

1. Do you like yourself? Why or why not?

2. Do you think you deserve to feel good about yourself? Why or why not?

3. What do you actually want for yourself and your life - your health, your physical body, your mind, your self-confidence, relationships, your career, your future, and your legacy to your family or the world? Make a list, a dream sheet, of the best version of yourself and your life as you envision it.

4. What positive changes can you begin to make in your life to start moving forward towards the best version of a life that you imagine for yourself?

5. Can you think of some experiences with your friends, co-workers, partners, or other people outside your family of origin, group or tribe, that have negatively impacted your self-confidence? List one to three of them in your journal.

6. Can you think of at least one positive result that came from each of those experiences?

MANIFEST

Stay seated and set your timer for five minutes. Answer question number one and then come back later to answer the other questions as time permits. Set your intention to manifest and keep moving forward towards the best version of your life as you envision it!

1. In your journal, make a list of all the things you want for yourself and your life: physically, mentally, emotionally, intellectually, relationally, professionally, financially, spiritually. This is the part of the book where I'm going to ask you to dream BIG! Just for a moment, imagine that anything was possible. If that were the case, what would you really wish for in all areas of your life?

2. Next, make a list of the realistic and specific positive steps that would need to occur in order for you to start moving in the direction of that best version of yourself and your life.

3. Re-read and focus on these goals daily and watch for the opportunities, people, and resources that will start to appear in your life in order to help you move forward in your journey. Mark each item off as it manifests in your life.

4. It's probably not going to happen overnight for most people, so prepare your mind. You can't control the circumstances of your life, but you can choose to flip the script and start telling yourself more empowering stories about the occasional negative life experiences that may come during your journey. Decide how those lessons will help you show up in a way that keeps you moving forward!

PRACTICE

The Yoga Mindset in REAL TIME:

Today, or anytime you wish to set and accomplish a goal that will lead you to the better version of yourself or your life, practice the Yoga Mindset in real time!

1. **MOVE:** Inhale slowly for five to six counts and exhale slowly for five to six counts and stand grounded and tall in Mountain Pose with your core sealed tightly.
2. **MEDITATE:** Declare: "Life is not happening *to* me, life is happening *for* me."
3. **MANIFEST:** Visualize yourself prioritizing your health and caring for yourself. See yourself as a healthy, competent, and confident person in all areas of your life and then act on your intention to start making the positive changes needed that will keep you moving forward to the best version of your life as you envision it. Let yourself feel what it would be like to practice extravagant self care daily and to set and achieve goals that help you move forward to all you want in life.

Yoga Mindset Principle #3:
I have the right to set and achieve my goals.
The Yoga Mindset Mantra:
Life is not happening *to* me, life is happening *for* me.

Change your mindset, change your life!

CHAPTER 4

I Love

"Please call me by my true name
so I can wake up,
and so the door of my heart can be left open,
the door of compassion."

Thich Nhat Hanh

One of the more memorable mind-altering projects that got our creative juices flowing in architecture school was to create a color spectrum from torn pieces of magazine pages. Our job was to complete the spectrum on a large roll of sketching paper about three feet wide by one hundred feet long. It was a brilliant project that not only taught us the principles of the color wheel, but also forced all of the summer intensive students to start connecting, communicating, and collaborating with each other as a team. It was the perfect introduction to what it is like to work in an architecture firm with different people.

There were about fifty of us in the summer intensive cohort, and we were divided into several groups - The red group, the orange group, and so on. While we were familiar with the many colors in a large crayon box, I think it's safe to say that few of us knew that there were about a bajillion gradations of every one of those colors. From red to purple-red, to red-orange, for example. We quickly realized that attention to that subtle detail, in one direction or the other, made for a successful, or failed, transition. We had one week to figure it out and complete the task.

There were many intense discussions and passionate disagreements, sometimes until 2 a.m. in the morning, about which color or which shade of a color should actually be next in the collage. Transitions between color groups became an even larger debate as the edges of one group approached the other. There were large swaths of white space to be covered by each group, so we had to focus not only on where we were working at the time but also on our final destination. It sounds a lot like the process of planning out an architectural design project, doesn't it? Our professors were so sneaky and clever.

As the week progressed, like the story of *The Little Red Hen*, we quickly figured out who actually did the work versus who did the talking and armchair coaching. When one color group finished, most everyone pitched in to help the other teams. Through it all, we witnessed the creation of our vision for a massive rainbow take shape on the paper rolled out on our long studio floor, and, more importantly, we witnessed connections between the students take place. We were no longer strangers to one another.

On the last day of the project, we all stood back and marveled at what we'd done together. We were ready for our presentation. The first-year design studio professors were routinely eccentric and ethereal in their lectures and one on one reviews of our work, but I noticed that they were waxing a bit more poetic than normal on presentation day. Something was up. By the time they got to the green section of the collage, they were geeking out about the depth of the colors, and I instantly realized what was going on. To this day, I can't prove it, but I think they were completely stoned. I couldn't help laughing out loud. While it was, admittedly, unprofessional and disrespectful to show up buzzed for a presentation, it was also hilarious, but not everyone understood what was going on.

From the back of the group, I noticed a very confident, fit, blonde-haired student who was clearly irritated and annoyed with their odd behavior and their obsession with the color green. He was making an intelligent point about something related to the project and arguing with the professors. In frustration, he looked around the room to see if anyone else agreed with his point. I'll never forget his sky blue eyes. I don't know if he actually saw me, but his glance was absolutely breathtaking. I was so impressed by his confidence, and, to be completely honest, he was pretty easy on the eyes. However, as quickly as I thought all of that to myself, I just as quickly shook those thoughts out of my head. I felt like I had come too far since Jake, so I moved on.

A couple of days later, while I was working intently at my desk, I heard a voice across from me say, "What is this?" I looked up and looked right into those sky blue eyes again. It felt like the whole building shook, but again, I caught myself and cemented my resolve not to fall again.

He was pointing to my deskmate's project, opposite my desk, with a quizzical look on his face. In an intentionally disinterested and slightly annoyed tone. I shrugged my shoulders and said, "I don't know." Without waiting for his reply, I looked back down and started working on my project again. He didn't leave. Instead, he asked another question. I looked up slowly and noticed he was smiling from ear to ear. I replied to his next question, and again, without waiting for his reply, I dropped my gaze and went back to work. He still didn't leave. This time, he planted himself firmly in the empty chair opposite my desk and kept talking. I looked up and saw that he was comfortably and confidently popping a wheelie in the chair opposite my desk, trying to engage me in conversation. His legs were spread open wide on either side of the chair, and he was holding on to the edge of the desk with one hand.

Balancing on the back two legs of the chair and smiling, I could see that he was feeling confident and that he was definitely flirting with me. I was cordial and polite but not encouraging. He was working hard to find a crack in my armor. I was definitely attracted and liked his determination, but I was resisting.

Around the time that I was getting ready to tell him that I really needed to get back to my work, I noticed that he had started to lean back a little too far. His fingers started to drift from the edge of the desk, and with his legs still spread wide on either side of the chair, I saw his confident smile and twinkling eyes switch to a gasping mouth and wide eyes as he realized he was at the point of no return.

In the time that it took me to stand up, he found the balancing point on the back two feet of the chair and hovered there for a moment. Like a man on a high wire without a pole, he was dancing on the two back feet of that chair when something even more unexpected happened. He farted. I'm not talking about a squeaker, folks. Nope, I'm talking about a long, drawn out, magnanimous, and clearly pronounced fart. Completely caught off guard by his unexpected flatulence, his struggling core gave way, and he was now in total free fall. I couldn't decide whether to hold out my 36" ruler as a lifeline or to give way to the laughter that was rising up inside of me as a result of that unexpected toot. I'm telling you, the internal conflict was *real* in the space of seconds.

His chair flew back, and as soon as his feet touched the floor mid-fall, he hurled his body forward, slamming into the opposite side of my desk. Standing across from him, startled and barely able to process all that had occurred, I hardly knew what to say or do next. That same look of bewilderment covered his beet red face, too. The awkward pause quickly gave way to uncontrollable laughter on both sides of the desk. We were laughing so hard that we were crying. In that moment of deep belly laughing, all my defenses came crashing down.

His efforts at flirting and trying to make a smooth move through standard male machismo and flattery had failed miserably. Still, this happy accident, this unanticipated bird dance on the chair in the wild for a mate, and the surprising bubbly punctuation to the mating ritual was just the divine intervention needed to cause the tiniest crack of compassion in my self-protective armor.

I really felt for this guy and wanted to help him out of a most awkward situation, but there was no easy way out except to share an unfiltered laugh together. That was just what I needed to open up my heart again. How long it had been since I'd laughed that hard and long.

Anodea Judith expressed that feeling so well when she wrote that, "compassion dissolves judgment and keeps hearts open. It's open widest by giving to another. When we love, we give from a place of abundance, not neediness. We expect nothing in return."

All pretense was gone between us. While I wanted to help restore him, he was actually helping to restore me. Neither of us expected anything in return. In my mind, I thought to myself, *I like this guy. The playing field has been leveled, and there is nowhere to go but up from here for both of us.*

Bonded deeply upon that first fart, we became fast and close friends. In fact, we became best friends long before we became intimate, and that gave us time to really get to know each other. We took a lot of time to build a solid and stable foundation of trust, support, and respect for each other.

Eventually, love began to grow for both of us. I was caught off guard when he shared his true feelings. There was a moment of hesitation on my part before I replied. Not because I felt otherwise, but because there was still a tiny piece of me that remembered the experience with Jake, and that tiny piece of me was terrified of being hurt so deeply again. Then, I came back to the present moment. I remembered that my memories and experiences were in the past and that the person opening his heart to me was actually real, very different, and in my present. I decided to take a chance again.

I opened up my heart and let love in again. I told him that I shared his sentiments. The truth of the matter was that I'd fallen for him long before I ever spoke the words. I just needed to take that final step of allowing love in. According to Anodea Judith, at the core of successful relationships is the ability to "allow love in… being fully present for someone, sharing yourself, opening to an unconditional acceptance of another's beingness."

I knew that there were no guarantees in love, but I decided to take that risk. It was the best uncalculated risk I have ever taken because it led me to my best friend, my soulmate, and the person who would eventually become my husband. It's funny how things work out, isn't it?

The Dalai Lama said to "remember that not getting what you want is sometimes a wonderful stroke of luck." I thought I wanted Jake, but I didn't get that. Had I never gone through what I did with Jake, had I never moved to Charlottesville, had I never applied to Virginia Tech, or to the School of Architecture, my now husband and I would never have met each other, and we would have missed the miracle. Though it felt like life was happening to me in the worst possible ways up to that point, in retrospect, it was also happening for me. Easy to see and say on the back side. Not so easy when you are in the middle of the storm. That takes a step of faith!

We dated all five years of college, and we were inseparable, but this time in a healthy way. We weren't lost without each other, but we were happier and more fulfilled when we were together. During the fourth year of architecture school, I moved to Paris for a six-month internship in a French architecture firm. What an unforgettable experience to be young, single and free in the streets and museums of Paris at the age of twenty-three. It still feels like a beautiful dream. The food, the language, the culture, the wine, the people, and 8 Rue Gassendi in the 11th Arrondissement will always hold a special place in my heart. All those years of studying French paid off. The only drawback was too much distance from my boyfriend.

When I returned to the US, the reunion was sweet, and Dan was quick to say that he never wanted to be away from me that long again.

Two months later, by the lights of the San Antonio Riverwalk at night, he proposed.

We graduated from college in May of 1990, and he was commissioned into the Navy that same week. One week later, we were married and quickly shipped off to his first Navy school in Coronado, California, where the next chapter of our life would begin.

As strange as it sounds, I thank God for my father's untimely death, my parent's marriage, my mom's struggles with mental health, and my devastating relationship with Jake. On the one hand, I wish all of the pain could have been bypassed, but had it not happened the way it did, I wouldn't have ended up where I am today. I couldn't say any of this when it was happening. I could barely function back then. I would have laughed, or possibly screamed, at anyone who told me to trust that all of it was working for me.

We can't control people or painful circumstances, but we can look for the lessons in those experiences and choose our response. We can choose to start telling ourselves new and empowering stories that help us heal and move forward. It's all a matter of courageously opening our heart to the possibilities before us again and again and again.

There are no guarantees that your heart won't be crushed again, but it might be worth the risk. Could you step out in faith, trusting that no matter what happens, life is happening for you? If you can get this in your heart, you can laugh at the most challenging storms in life, knowing that at some point, in the future, this side of heaven, Lord willing, you may understand and see how it was working for you.

Even when you can't see how it could possibly be working for you in the moment of trauma or devastation, it's vitally important to tell yourself that life is always happening for you. Once you get this rooted deeply in your heart, no matter what happens, no matter how hard it is, fear can more easily and quickly be pushed aside and left in the past as you move forward towards the life of your dreams. It's all in your mindset!

The Yoga Mindset Formula, Day 4

MOVE

**Mountain Pose Alignment Principle #4: Open your Heart
Set your timer for five minutes and move!**

The Chest & Back

1. Set your foundation, move the shins forward, pull the thighs back, contract the muscles of your thighs to stand tall. Add that knee-saving micro-bend. Bring the pelvis to neutral and seal the core.
2. Rotate the triceps towards the back. Hug both of the shoulder blades towards the spine and then shift them down slightly. Feel the change in your chest, and imagine the heart opening in the process. This motion integrates, stabilizes, and protects the shoulder from injury and allows us to open our chest, contract our shoulder blades and stand taller.

It's interesting to consider that intuitively, before most people pick up a heavy piece of luggage, they will first ground their feet, soften their knees, tuck their tailbone slightly, seal their core, rotate their triceps towards the back, and retract their shoulder blades. Sound familiar? It's Mountain Pose. See, you were already mastering the pose and didn't even know it.

It is a subconscious patterning in our body that kicks in when we lift anything heavy. It's the same in our posture. Some of us stand tall and confident, but many more hunch over, lost in our phones, or our work, or our emotions. When you practice Mountain Pose, however, you start to reverse those closed upper body patterns. You may notice a new shift in how you feel about your body, yourself, and your life overall when you start standing tall, with your heart open, in Mountain Pose.

As you start to implement these upper body movements, your upper back may be a bit sore. Take it slowly and shift gently. Keep your shoulders broad, and your heart lifted up as you go through your day. Standing tall and lifting the heart probably sounds easy to most people, but if you've ever been in a closed or protective position for a long period of time, shifting to a more upright and open position may feel like a journey of a thousand miles. If that is you, take it one step at a time. Notice how your body changes during the day. Do you hunch over in certain situations or when certain people are around? What connections can you make between your emotions and your body in those situations, if that is the case? Are the relationships toxic, or is it more a matter of your self-confidence? Whatever the case, the effect of standing tall will be profound. Your heart will be lifted to the world again, and in that position, standing tall with your heart open, you'll be able to see so much more and so much more clearly.

Breathwork: Inhale slowly for five to six counts and exhale slowly for five to six counts for each breath below.

Breath 1: Set your foundation and quietly declare to yourself, "I am," and "I have the right to be here."

Breath 2: Bring your pelvis to neutral and quietly declare to yourself, "I feel," and "I have the right to feel, both emotionally and physically."

Breath 3: Seal your core and quietly declare to yourself, "I do," and "I have the right to set goals and accomplish them."

Breath 4: Lift your heart to the world again and quietly declare to yourself, "I have the right to give and receive love."

Breath 5: Declare to yourself, "Life is not happening TO me. Life is happening FOR me."

To what degree can you walk in love for yourself and others today, knowing full well the risks and rewards? Knowing that it may or may not be reciprocated, and might even be rejected, depending on the circumstances, will it be worth the risk or potential reward? Only you can answer that question. You always have the choice.

MEDITATE

Set your timer for five minutes and answer questions six and seven below as you consider where you are in the process of giving and receiving love in your relationships. Come back later to answer the other questions as time permits.

1. Who are the people that you are very fond of beyond your family of origin?
2. Which ones on that list are easy to love? Why do you think it's so easy?
3. Which ones on that list are difficult to love? Why do you think it's so difficult?
4. Knowing that you can't control people or circumstances, how can you change yourself or show up in those relationships differently today to give and receive more love?
5. What changes would that require within yourself? Is the relationship worth it to you?
6. Are there relationships beyond your family of origin that have broken your heart in the past? List them in your journal.
7. Can you think of at least one positive result that came from each of those negative experiences?

MANIFEST

Set your timer for five more minutes and answer question number five below. Come back later to complete the rest of the questions, as time permits.

1. Make a list of the people who are easy to love in your life, beyond your family of origin.
2. Make a list of the people who are difficult to love in your life, beyond your family of origin.
3. Ask the people who are easy to love how you can love them better and then take action. Write the goal next to each person's name. Cross it off when done.
4. Consider what you could do for the people who are difficult to love (maybe from a distance, if being with them would be an unsafe situation) and then take action. Write the goal next to each person's name. Cross it off when done.
5. How can you show up differently in intimate relationships moving forward as a result of the positives you may have found in the negative experiences of your past intimate relationships?

PRACTICE

The Yoga Mindset in REAL TIME

Today, or anytime you feel a desire to open your heart to give and receive love, take action with the Yoga Mindset in real time!

1. **MOVE:** Inhale slowly for five to six counts and exhale slowly for five to six counts and stand in Mountain Pose with your shoulders retracted towards the spine and down and heart lifted to the world.
2. **MEDITATE:** Declare to yourself: "Life is not happening *to* me, life is happening *for* me."
3. **MANIFEST:** Visualize yourself "showing up" in a different way in your intimate relationships moving forward in order to give and receive more love. Let yourself feel what that would be like in reality. See it in your mind's eye. Remember to only follow through in person if it is safe for you and all parties involved. If not safe, consider how you can show up from a distance.

Yoga Mindset Principle #4:
I have the right to give and receive love.
The Yoga Mindset Mantra:
Life is not happening *to* me, life is happening *for* me.

Change your mindset, change your life!

CHAPTER 5

I Speak

*"It's not about finding your voice,
it's about giving yourself permission
to use your voice."*

Kris Carr

After observing the challenges of my parent's marriage, I wanted to try to do things a bit differently. I felt like my chances of marital success were high based not only on the love Dan and I had for each other but also on his unbelievably balanced and healthy family of origin. He was the most grounded, confident, kind, handsome, smart, talented, honest, fun, funny, principled, faithful man I knew. I definitely had him on a pedestal. He could do no wrong and all of that goodness was spilling over into me and our marriage daily.

We had been married for about six months when we were transferred to our first "duty station." A few months after our arrival, and several rounds of anthrax shots for my husband, he set out on his first deployment in August of 1991. I was a new bride, and he was headed to the Middle East for Operation Desert Storm. He was going to war. I wondered if he'd be okay. I wondered if we'd be okay. I wondered if he'd even come home again.

I wasn't prepared for all the what-ifs. My mind was reeling, but as most military spouses do, as the departure date crept closer, I created just enough friction between us to make the separation easier and then put on a brave face to hide the broken heart as he boarded the ship.

Military life with a spouse coming and going for six months at a time is a different kind of emotional rollercoaster. Nonetheless, I felt that we could make it through anything. I hoped and prayed for the best, but honestly had no idea what to expect as a new Navy spouse.

Back in the 90s, personal computers for email and easy access to cell phones didn't exist for most people. Instead, we made calls on actual phones, hard-wired into a building or a public telephone booth, and we wrote letters. I still have shoeboxes full of all those letters. If ever there was a fire in my home, and there was time, I would probably grab those shoeboxes full of love.

During deployments in 1991, communications were very limited. Mail would be air-dropped onto a ship occasionally or collected at various ports of call around the world. Calls would come when a payphone could be found abroad, but they were few and far between. The handwritten letters came a bit more frequently, and they kept me afloat.

The days were long and quiet in the house that suddenly seemed so big. I adopted a dog from the local shelter and she was the best dog I've ever had. She was just the companion I needed at that time.

When not hanging out with Sophie, I wrote my husband juicy letters dripping with the passion of a new and lonely wife in her mid-twenties. His letters were just as passionate, but then I noticed they dropped off significantly around mid-deployment. I started to feel a bit neglected as I listened to the other spouses at meetings talk about their letters that somehow kept showing up in their mailboxes. I tried not to overthink it and assumed only the best. When we finally spoke on the phone again, I asked what was going on. He apologized and said he was just crazy busy. I believed him.

I had thoroughly enjoyed my two years off as a new bride after graduating from college, working architecture jobs here and there, but now, I was bored out of my mind, watching TV and eating way too many chips and salsa. With some extra pounds on my body, I was feeling out of shape and decided that something had to change. I started applying for full-time jobs in the area and after a lot of cold calls and sending out a small armada of resumes, I was eventually offered a position with the Army Corps of Engineers as an architect.

I progressed through the ranks quickly and was enjoying the life of an architect without all the responsibilities of having to make dinner for somebody every night, but I missed my husband terribly.

As his letters and calls continued to fall off, I went from feeling sad and confused to feeling neglected and angry. We started growing apart. When the deployment finally ended, and we were reunited, in a quiet moment, I asked again why his letters and calls evaporated. After a long and quiet pause, he shared that the deployment was rough. He said that he was getting little to no sleep and that the stress was high. It was starting to affect him and the crew in strange ways. Apparently, it was so bad that at one point, a crew member put a gun to his head during some training to "drive home" a point. I couldn't believe what I was hearing, but then again, it was a time of war with so much tension and so many unknowns.

After a long talk about all that happened for both of us during the deployment, we realized that between six-month deployments, plus shorter underway periods and numerous training days, his three and a half years in the Navy had resulted in him being gone about seventy-five percent of our married life. Distance, long separations, and war had taken their toll on both of us. We were finally together, and yet, miles apart.

A few weeks later, he told me that he was due for a transfer soon and asked if I'd like to help him make the wish list for possible duty stations. I declined and instead told him to go ahead and make the list himself.

Several weeks after that, he told me he'd be transferring to Italy after a brief stint in Monterey, California, where he'd learn Italian at the Defense Language Institute. He asked me to join him, but by then, we'd grown even farther apart, so I declined his offer. Instead, I handed him divorce papers.

Shocked, his temper flared, with mine rising just as quickly. We both found our raw and unedited voices, and after several rounds of heated arguments, to drive home his point, my husband hurled one of our wedding gifts, a Noritake crystal goblet, against our living room wall.

94

The sight and sound of the glass shattering against the wall, a summary of the state of our marriage, brought me to tears.

The tension in the house was beyond painful for the next couple of weeks. Angry words and short tempers were the norm. Eventually, the time came for him to leave. He had decided to take a solo bike ride down the West Coast, a seven hundred mile trip to Monterey, California. Right before he left, I offered up the papers one last time, but again, he refused. I watched him ride away until I couldn't see him anymore.

During the separation, we spoke on the phone periodically and started individual counseling. That was such an eye-opener for me. I was so close to the issues that I couldn't see or think clearly about any of it, but a third, unbiased, outside observer helped me to untangle the knot of myself in the situation one strand at a time. With her insightful observations, thought-provoking questions, and gentle suggestions, I was able to see things more clearly and work through my own issues in the situation. I was able to take an honest look at myself, and that was key to making headway.

With the counselor's guidance, I realized that I still loved my husband very much and that I still wanted to be with him more than anyone else in the entire world, no matter what had occurred during the multiple separations. We'd married for better or for worse. This was the worse part. Once I decided what I really wanted, and spoke it, little things started happening all around me, undeniably confirming my decision to restore the relationship.

I started going to church again, and slowly, grace, healing, and hope flowed back into my soul. I continued counseling and spent more time with family and friends, good friends, the kind who walk with you, side by side, softly whispering hope into seemingly impossible situations.

Forgiveness started rising up in the place where fear and hopelessness had taken root. Eventually, I recovered my voice again, only this time, I didn't use it to speak division. I used it to speak about restoration. I called my husband and told him that I was finally ready to come to California, if the offer still stood.

I took a leave of absence from work, packed my bags, and hit the road with the band, Alphaville, leading me on. Coming back together was not easy. In fact, it felt more like a head-on collision. There were many arguments and a lot of tears as we worked through the issues, but eventually, there was supernatural healing. We did the hard work of learning to see each other in a new way, as we were, altered by the time apart, and then we did the even harder work of rebuilding the trust and healing a broken marriage.

Slowly, with a deep and intimate connection to God, we were drawn back to each other. We found that the love was still there, deep inside, and over time, we were able to reconnect, realign and move forward together again.

I returned to Seattle, put in my two weeks notice, and started the transition process. We were reunited in Seattle in November when his language training was done. We celebrated Thanksgiving at Burger King, and it was the best and most memorable Thanksgiving that I've ever shared with anyone. We were like newlyweds again, practically joined at the hip to each other.

We renewed our wedding vows in a small intimate ceremony with a few family members and some very close friends that never gave up hope on us. That wedding ceremony was more meaningful and memorable than our first wedding. We packed up, moved out, and set off for our next adventure in Italy. We felt like newlyweds, and the future felt wide open to us again.

Quieting all the other voices in my head and resigning from my job was the best decision I ever made, but I had to know what I really wanted for myself and my future in order to make those changes. I had to get to a point where I was ready to share myself as I was and to see my husband as he was and I had to use my voice to declare it. An article by Hannah Leatherbury reiterated that point when she wrote that, "You are meant to share yourself just as you are – your strengths and your beauty along with your vulnerabilities and your blemishes."

I needed to use my voice to say what I wanted without worrying about what anyone thought about me, my career or my future. Next, I had to act. I had to start making the necessary changes to move in the direction of the life I envisioned for myself. I didn't have all the answers, and I didn't know how it would all work out, but I trusted God to take care of all the details.

My husband and I have faced more challenges throughout the years, and we've let each other down more times than I care to mention, but the love grows stronger and deeper, and forgiveness comes more quickly now.

As crazy as it sounds, that hell-on-earth experience so early in our marriage helped us see each other as we actually were, blemishes and all, and it made us stronger and better. More importantly, it helped us both decide if we were committed to each other for better or for worse. We were.

The healing that took place in our marriage was nothing short of miraculous, but something even more miraculous resulted from our marital struggles. Though it wasn't easy, sharing our story with other married couples helped them step out of the shadows and share similar struggles. Speaking about our story gave us instant access into the lives of other couples, also teetering on the edge of separation or divorce.

Over the years, we've been blessed to share our experiences and to use our voices to speak hope and healing into their lives. We have encouraged married couples to remember their commitment for better or for worse and to seek wise counseling when it's worse. We never cease to be amazed at how God still works miracles in seemingly impossible situations when we are willing to use our voice for good in the world.

There is incredible power in your voice and in expressing yourself and your story. If speaking is difficult for you, "bringing balance to the expressive energy found in your throat...will deepen your ability to speak about and act upon your deepest truths," according to Hannah Leatherbury. How do you find the balance? Search your heart. What are you passionate about? What matters most to you? Health, wellness, freedom, self-care, equal opportunity, service to others, faith, family, or other issues? You know yourself best. Give yourself permission to speak about the things you are passionate about and branch out from there.

On your own, in the privacy of your own home, you have the power to speak the best version of your life into the being at all times. The results may not happen instantly, but over time, perhaps some, or all, of those declarations may come to pass. There are no guarantees in life, but you'll never know until you try. So, try it. Take a deep breath and speak out loud what you dream for yourself, your health, your family, your relationships, your career, your marriage, your children, your legacy, your community, your nation, the world, your purpose, and your future. Give yourself permission to declare it every single day. Better yet, say it while you look into a mirror. Write it down in your journal. Look at it weekly and note any people or situations that help you get you closer to that future. Most importantly, let yourself feel that reality. Imagine it. Visualize it. See it in your mind's eye as real and perhaps, one day, it may be.

Don Miguel Ruiz wrote that "your word is the power that you have to create. Your word is the gift that comes directly from God… Through the word, you express your creative power. It is through the word that you manifest everything. Regardless of what language you speak, your intent manifests through the word. What you dream, what you feel, and what you really are will all be manifested through the word. The word is not just a sound or a written symbol. The word is a force; it is the power you have to express and communicate, to think, and thereby to create the events in your life."

So speak about the magic inside of you. This is not from a place of ego, but from a place of seeing value in yourself and your thoughts to make a situation better. Speak up in staff meetings and in your relationships. Your words matter. Articulate what you want and what you need. You may not get it, but you surely won't get it if you don't at least try to articulate what you want.

Celebrate every failure and every bit of progress as forward motion. Consider what changes you may need to make in order to keep moving towards your best future. Make a plan, take action and watch for the miracle.

The Yoga Mindset Formula, Day 5

MOVE

Mountain Pose Alignment Principle #5: Breathe Deeply!
Set your timer for five minutes and move!

The Throat, Lungs & Breathwork

1. Set your foundation, shins forward, thighs back, legs strong, and standing tall. Add that knee-saving micro bend, bring the pelvis to neutral, and seal the core. Rotate the triceps towards the back. Hug the shoulder blades towards the spine and down, open your heart, lift your chin and open your throat. Allow your breath and voice to flow freely.

2. Holding that position, sweep your arms up over your head as you inhale through your nose for five to six slow counts, pause for five to six counts at the top of your inhale and quietly say to yourself "I have the right to speak and be heard," and then sweep your arms down to your sides as you exhale through your nose for five to six slow counts and pause at the bottom of your exhale for five to six counts. If five to six slow counts make you feel a little claustrophobic, try three breaths up and down to start and work towards five breaths at your own pace. Repeat this breath pattern three or more times until the five minute segment is completed.

Have you ever considered how closely the breath is tied to both emotions and the physical body? Have you ever noticed that your body becomes tense if you are upset or angry, and your breath usually becomes short, irregular, and shallow? Our issues are in our tissues. As a result of that state of being, our voice is usually compromised, as well.

On the other hand, if we are calm, our body relaxes, and our breath becomes long, regular, and deep. As a result of this state of being, our voice is usually steady, grounded, and strong.

In yoga, the goal is always to align the breath with the movement. First and foremost, as we synchronize our slow deep breaths with movement, it calms our sympathetic system (the flight or fight response) and activates the parasympathetic nervous system (the rest and digest response).

When the parasympathetic nervous system is activated, we are able to be more relaxed and present to all that is actually occurring around us, instead of being forever lost in thoughts of past and future and the related reactions. If you think about it a while, the past is gone. It was real, but in many ways, it is a memory from the point of view of the present. It's the same with our future. We aren't even there yet, so in many ways, it's an illusion that has not yet come to pass.

Ironically, most people spend incredible energy and time obsessing and ruminating about the past and worrying about things that may happen in the future but usually don't. Present moment awareness is heightened as we focus on our slow deep breathing, however. It helps us stay rooted in the now and helps us to see things as they are right in front of us. With focused breathwork, we can move from a place of reaction to a place of intentional responding to create the best version of our lives, moment by moment.

"A last word on slow breathing. It goes by another name: prayer," according to James Nestor, the author of the recent and incredible book, *Breathe.* He goes on to say that "When Buddhist monks chant their most popular mantra, each spoken phrase lasts six seconds, with six seconds to inhale before the chant starts again. The Sa Ta Na Ma chant, one of the best-known techniques in Kundalini yoga, also takes six seconds to vocalize, followed by six seconds to inhale. In the ancient Hindu khechari, each takes six seconds. Japanese, African, Hawaiian, Native American, Buddhist, Taoist, Christian - these cultures and religions all have somehow developed the same prayer techniques, requiring the same breathing patterns. Patricia Gerbarg, MD, and Richard P. Brown, MD have written books and published several scientific articles about the restorative power of slow breathing, which would become known as 'resonant breathing.' In many ways, this breathing offered the same benefits as meditation for people who didn't want to meditate. Or yoga, for people who didn't like to get off the couch. It offered the healing touch of prayer for people who weren't religious. Did it matter if we breathed at a rate of six or five seconds or were a half-second off? It did not when practiced at 5.5 breaths a minute."

"We believe that the rosary may have partly evolved because it synchronized with the inherent cardiovascular (Mayer) rhythms, and this gave a feeling of wellbeing..." the Pavia researchers wrote. "In other words, the meditations, Ave Marias, and dozens of other prayers that had been developed over the past several thousand years weren't all baseless. Prayer heals, especially when it's practiced at 5.5 breaths a minute." That works out to approximately five to six slow breaths of a five to six count inhale and a five to six count exhale, and that is exactly why we include breathwork in the movement segment of the Yoga Mindset. It is based on thousands of years of practice, and apparently, it works!

Your five minutes of movement and breathwork every day will help calm your nervous system, so always remember to breathe first when applying the Yoga Mindset to any stressful situation. Inhale slowly through the nose for five to six counts and exhale slowly through the nose for five to six counts. Aim to get at least one breath in before an exciting or difficult situation arises, and if you have a full minute, get as many slow breaths as possible.

MEDITATE

Take a seat, set your timer for five minutes, and answer questions six and seven below. Come back later to answer the other questions as time permits.

1. Do you feel like your voice is clear and strong or more hesitant and weak, in general?
2. Is it difficult for you to verbally state your needs without guilt or to establish healthy boundaries in all areas of your life today? Why or why not?
3. Do you believe that you have the right to speak and be heard regarding the things that matter to you? Why or why not?
4. What are the issues that you are passionate about in your life?
5. How can you use your voice today to move towards speaking more boldly about the things that matter to you?
6. Can you think of one to three times when you, or someone else, suppressed your voice? List them in your journal.
7. Can you think of at least one positive result that came from each of those negative experiences?

MANIFEST

Set your timer for five minutes, answer question three below, and start to flip the script on the negative stories you may have been telling yourself about your voice. Come back later to answer the other questions as time permits.

In addition to deciding to use your voice for what you want most for yourself or someone else, we will also occasionally need to have some difficult conversations.

Have you ever had to confront a friend, break up with someone, disagree with a coworker, confront an employee or possibly fire someone? Those are difficult conversations, but they are necessary from time to time. It's so much easier to avoid these tough conversations altogether, but like trying to avoid looking at the proverbial "elephant in the room," the issue never really goes away. In fact, the issue usually gets bigger and more complicated when left unaddressed. Confrontation is so challenging for most people, but some people excel at it. I once met a gentleman who said he loved confrontation because it meant he, someone else, or his group were getting better. Interesting perspective, but not exactly easy. A cheat sheet comes in handy.

Below are some suggestions that may help you find your voice in confrontational situations. It's important to remember that you are a perfectly imperfect vessel speaking to another perfectly imperfect vessel as you go into these conversations. It's equally important to remember that you, and they, have the right to speak and be heard. Ensure you have your turn to speak and then allow them their turn, too.

When you try to have an adult discussion, where everyone can voice their opinion or feelings, there will occasionally be some people that will treat you poorly until you speak up and teach them how to treat you well.

Emotions will be high during difficult conversations. In those moments, remember to breathe. Remember what I said earlier about slow deep breathing as a gateway to calm? Remind yourself that the goal of confrontation is not to crush someone, but to clarify a misunderstanding, express something important, improve a relationship, improve performance or improve a situation for a multitude of other reasons that will eventually benefit everyone involved. It's a way to get better together.

1. What do you want most for yourself and your life? Can you speak it out loud?

2. What changes would you need to make to start moving in the direction of your best life where you can speak freely?

3. Is there a difficult discussion you need to have with someone? Only you know the best timing. Take some time in advance to write out what the issues are, and consider, step by step, what you will say to that person. Also, take a very hard look at yourself in this process and identify the part, great or small, that you may have played and own it.

4. When you meet, aim to ease a tense situation by thanking the person for meeting you.

5. Next, let them know that you've been giving the specific matter a lot of thought, and then use your voice to state whatever part you may have played in the equation. It usually takes two to tango. This will hopefully help them see that you value self-reflection, honesty, and taking personal responsibility. It may also make them feel like they too can own their part in the

situation. Hopefully, it will also help them shift their mindset from defensiveness to open discussion and collaboration to resolve the issue.

6. State the purpose of the meeting, and explain the impact their choices or behavior had on you, the family, or the team. Talk about the way it made you, the family, or the team feel, and then let them talk. They may try to justify their actions, make excuses or blame others. Their words may completely trigger you. Say nothing. Just notice the emotion you may be feeling. Remember the Yoga Mindset Formula: BREATHE! Five to six counts in and five to six counts out. Plant your feet, seal your core, open your heart, and quietly remind yourself that you, and the other person, have the right to speak and be heard.

7. Listen carefully. Really focus on the other person. Try to imagine yourself in their shoes. Try to see it from their point of view. Then, if you can see their logic, confirm that you can see why or how they might have felt this way or that way, or done this or that, given the situation, their unique personality or point of view. Then restate the main issue and its impact on you, the family, or the team, and restate the desire to find a better way forward so that it doesn't happen again. Keep repeating these words over and over again for as long as they keep explaining or defending themselves and until you both agree upon a better way forward for all.

PRACTICE

The Yoga Mindset in REAL TIME

Today, or anytime, when you feel a desire to speak and be heard, take action with the Yoga Mindset in real time!

1. **MOVE:** Inhale slowly for five to six counts, exhale slowly for five to six counts, and stand in Mountain Pose with your chin lifted and throat open to allow your breath to flow freely. At the top and bottom of each breath, repeat to yourself, "I have the right to speak and be heard."

2. **MEDITATE:** Declare, "Life is not happening *to* me, life is happening *for* me."

3. **MANIFEST:** Visualize yourself not only finding your voice, but also giving yourself permission to use your voice about things that really matter to you. Let yourself feel how empowering it could be to be confident as a speaker. See yourself as that person. See yourself speaking up. Think about how you can flip the script on any negative stories you may have been telling yourself up to this point about your voice. Consider how you can "show up" differently in your life and others' lives with your voice.

Yoga Mindset Principle #5:
I have the right to speak and be heard.
The Yoga Mindset Mantra:
Life is not happening *to* me, life is happening *for* me.

Change your mindset, change your life!

CHAPTER 6

I See

"I was blind,
but now
I see."

John 9:25, The NIV Bible

On October 31, 2016, our family was transferred back to the United States after four years of living and working abroad in Singapore. Trust me when I say that it was more "trick" than "treat" to return to the US that particular Halloween. While we were overseas, our eldest son was at college studying architecture. Thanksgiving break was just around the corner, and a long-overdue and much-anticipated reunion with him was on the horizon. I couldn't wait to see him again.

He had been diagnosed with High Functioning Asperger Syndrome, or High-Functioning Autism, as it's now called, in middle school, but had made it through both high school and college with much support overseas. Physically and intellectually, he had no issues. In fact, he excelled in both of those areas at the Singapore American International School. Soft social and communication skills were another thing altogether, however.

For those who are not familiar with autism, it is a neurodevelopmental condition characterized by difficulties with social interaction and communication. Its symptoms range from mild to severe. "High-functioning autism is often used to refer to those on the milder end of the spectrum," according to Healthline.

All seemed to be going well for him until two weeks after our return to the U.S. I received a call from a nurse informing us that our son was at the local ER and that his heart rate was 34 bpm. She said that he was sedated and stable, but that we might want to get there as quickly as possible.

"Surely, there is some sort of mistake," I said in shock and disbelief. I had just spoken with him the day before. He said he was sad because he and his girlfriend had broken up, but he seemed as okay as someone can be when that happens. I asked the ER nurse for more information, but she said, "sorry, we can't tell you anything more because your son is now twenty-one and would need to give us permission for the details of his condition to be discussed." Shaking, but trying to keep it together, I asked in measured breaths, "How, exactly, would a sedated adult be able to do that?" The reply was like something out of a never-ending vicious do-loop.

The nurse kept repeating that she was very sorry, but that she couldn't tell us any more until our son gave her permission to do so. I again reminded her that he was sedated. She apologized again. That went on for about three rounds. I paused and decided to stop the insanity. I took a slow deep breath and then ended the conversation by letting her know that we would be there as quickly as possible.

We were still new to the area and stuffed like sardines into a tiny hotel room with four adults, eight suitcases, a cat, and one fragrant litter box. We had no car, no home, no church, no connections in our new area, and no idea what was really going on with our son. Shocked, worried, and confused, my mind was jumping to the absolute worst-case scenarios. The deep breathing was helping, but I had not yet gotten to flowing with the storm.

Two weeks into his new job, my husband had no choice but to contact his new supervisor and request time off. Not the best first impression, but the universe reminded me again that life is always working for us when his supervisor also shared that she had a special needs family member and understood completely.

He bought a same-day airline ticket for himself and our youngest son, a junior year at a new high school, with all the money we didn't have after a transcontinental move. We alternately cried and prayed all the way to the airport. Gordon MacDonald recommends to "let inward prayer be your last act before you fall asleep and the first act when you awake," but under the circumstances, prayer all day long was in order.

A quick kiss goodbye, and the car door slammed shut. I watched my husband and my sixteen-year-old son grow smaller as they walked towards the terminal. The quiet of the car was deafening, except for the sound of an airplane taking off in the distance. It made me think of the Baby Grasshopper yoga pose I'd been trying to master.

I drove back to the hotel on autopilot, where my equally distressed and concerned daughter would be waiting. Time passed so slowly between the calls from my husband updating me. Our son was in serious condition after what sounded like a breakdown. I prayed even harder and started asking others to lift him up in prayer, as well. There is great power in our voice and even more power in our focused and unified prayers and meditations for someone other than ourselves. There really is power in numbers.

I thought about doing some yoga to calm my mind, but at that moment, everything, even yoga, seemed so insignificant and unimportant. I thought about the Baby Grasshopper pose again and about how hard it was for me. I thought about gravity and about how it always made me feel stuck to the ground. Then, I thought of how emotionally heavy I felt at that moment. Actually, I felt more than heavy. I felt frozen and stuck.

I finally decided to walk across the street to a local hot yoga class. The instructor's words were just what I needed to hear. They helped me focus and calm my restless mind, and then she said, "Let's move on to Baby Grasshopper." I thought, "Not going to happen, but I'll try again." I set myself up, grabbed my foot, and started shifting forward onto one hand and one foot, but once again, gravity kept me down. I just couldn't get lift-off. The instructor saw me struggling and somehow knew what I needed. She gave me a look of encouragement, and I decided to attempt the lift one more time. Inhale, shift, lift, and then it happened. In one quick exhale, I nailed it!

I was positively elated, but how was it possible that at a time when my heart and mind were heavy enough to keep me grounded indefinitely, I was in the pose that a breath earlier seemed impossible? I told myself it was just luck, but I knew better. It was the result of a thousand times of trying and failing. It was the result of small, consistent, and focused efforts that ultimately led to success. It was also the result of the instructor's encouragement and guidance. I was hovering about a foot above the ground, but I felt like I'd broken through some invisible barrier in the atmosphere. Light and airy, gravity no longer held me down. I'd hung on and tried again, at the most difficult time. I found a way forward. I smiled at my success. Then I smiled as I saw the positive lesson in the moment.

Just as I had found a way forward in Baby Grasshopper, I instantly knew that we would also find a way forward with our son. We would get through this. Baby Grasshopper seemed so impossible for so long, but it had come to pass. The situation with my son also seemed impossible, but I knew that nothing was impossible with God, so I lifted up a prayer for the life and soul of my son.

Jim Downing wrote that "God clearly commanded the process of meditation. In His commission to Joshua, He said, 'This book of the law shall not depart from your mouth, but you shall meditate on it day and night, so that you may be careful to do according to all that is written in it.' It is evident that God has a great deal to say about meditation, considering it a vital exercise of the minds of His children." Lying there in the yoga studio during savasana, I took some time to quietly meditate on the thought that lift-off was possible for anyone.

I didn't know what to expect with our son, and I certainly didn't look forward to round two of dealing with mental illness. Still, I was comforted by the thought that I already knew what to expect. I was actually thoroughly prepared, having seen the worst of it with my mom as she battled mental illness over the years. When I considered all of this, I was able to quickly flip the script on those negative stories I was telling myself about my son and the negative stories I had told myself for years about my mother's mental illness. Once again, I was able to see that life had been happening for me. All the struggle and heartache, all of it, prepared me for this very moment.

With a grateful heart, I knew that we were going to be okay, and then, with a quiet joy rising in me, everything became blurry. Thankfully, it was still savasana in a hot yoga studio. This is the closing and relaxation pose of every yoga class, and in the heat, when you are drenched with sweat, it's hard to tell the difference between tears and sweat.

My husband made it back to Virginia with our son just in time for Thanksgiving. The young man that stepped out of the car was not the same one we'd dropped off at the start of that school year. We had no idea he was struggling so intensely because he was not the best at communicating with us. It was a slow road to recovery.

There were multiple doctor visits, counseling sessions, inpatient and outpatient psychiatric hospital stays, overmedicated, undermedicated, reconfirmations of high-functioning autism, and a diagnosis of a breakdown that neither the medical profession nor my son could fully explain, even to this day.

On this journey, I have learned so much. For instance, did you know that there is a massive mental health issue in America and the world, but there are not enough doctors to meet the need? I have also realized that there are so many people around me who also struggle with mental illness, including anxiety and depression. At the moment, we have a stable medical situation for my son, and we are so grateful, but we still take it day by day.

As I found the courage to share some of the struggles of living with someone battling mental health issues, I saw my extended family, friends, and colleagues start to open up about themselves, their families, or their friends and their respective struggles with mental health issues, too. These were people who I had known for years and yet, never really knew or "saw" completely.

I also realized that there is still a stigma attached to mental illness, but we can't keep quiet about it. It's real, and it's everywhere. These are people, hidden in plain sight, right in front of us, in desperate need of support, counseling, and possibly medication. We need only open our eyes and "see" them and, especially, those who support them.

The family members of people struggling with mental illness are also more than likely suffering and struggling to maintain balance in their lives, too. They are on the "front lines," and they are mentally, emotionally, physically, and often financially drained and exhausted. I speak from experience.

Thanks to a lot of love, prayer, and a commitment to finding the right medication, today, my son is stable and moving forward in his life again. We take it one day at a time. Like the instructor who helped me take flight with just one encouraging look from across the room, I keep whispering encouragement into my son's eyes, ears, heart, and soul for better days ahead.

I cherish every one of his attempts at getting back on track and celebrate every small, consistent effort because I know where it leads. It leads to lift-off. It leads to success. It will happen in his own time and in his own way. I can see it in my mind's eye, and I visualize it routinely, believing that his mind will be healed, gravity will release its grip on him, and he will lift off and soar once again. As I write this, it's all coming to pass.

Visualization expert Shakti Gawain reconfirmed the power of visualizing the results you desire when she wrote that "creative visualization is the technique of using your imagination to create what you want in your life...This is the principle that whatever you put out into the universe will be reflected back to you. As you sow, so shall you reap. What this means from a practical standpoint is that we always attract into our lives whatever we think about the most, believe in most strongly, expect on the deepest levels, and / or imagine most vividly. When we are negative and fearful, insecure or anxious, we often attract the very experiences, situations, or people we seek to avoid. If we are basically positive in attitude, expecting and envisioning pleasure, satisfaction, and happiness, we tend to attract and create people, situations, and events that conform to our positive expectations. So, consciously imagining what we want can help us manifest it in our lives." So, let's not waste another moment, let's practice!

The Yoga Mindset Formula, Day 6

MOVE

Mountain Pose Alignment Principle #6: Fix your gaze!
Set your timer for five minutes and move!

The Eyes & Breathwork

1. Set your foundation. Shins forward, thighs back, legs strong, and standing tall. Add that knee-saving micro bend, bring the pelvis to neutral, seal the core, rotate the triceps towards the back. Hug the shoulder blades towards the spine and down. Open your chest and lift your heart and inhale for five to six slow breaths and then exhale for five to six slow breaths. Repeat this one to three times.

2. Lift your gaze to look straight ahead. Pull the jawline back slightly so that the head is stacked squarely over the neck and spine. Find your focal point, about three feet, or a meter, in front of you. It can be anything, but it should be something that is not moving. Fix your eyes softly on that spot. Inhale for five to six slow counts as you sweep your arms up over your head, pause for five to six slow counts at the top of your breath and quietly say to yourself, "I have the right to see and be seen," then sweep your arms down to your sides as you exhale for five to six slow counts and pause at the bottom of your exhale for five to six counts while quietly repeating to yourself, "I have the right to see and be seen." Holding your gaze on your focal point the whole time,

repeat the breath and arm sweeping patterns three times or more, or until the five minute segment is complete.

Consider what you fix your eyes on in your life. Is it the most important thing in your life, or do you think you have lost sight of the big picture? Do you need to adjust your main focus? If so, what changes would be required?

MEDITATE

Take a seat, set your timer for five minutes, and answer question number one below. Come back later to answer question number two as time permits.

Did you know that, initially, yoga was more focused on the ability to quiet the mind than the yoga poses? Some people refer to the practice of quieting the mind and focusing on something as meditation. Others refer to it as prayer. Whatever you call it, it's been practiced and documented for thousands of years. We all get stuck in the past, and the future, in our minds, so easily and so often. How many times have you said, "Ugh, I should have done this or said that," or "I know that this meeting is not going to go well, or I know that something bad is going to happen." The mind spins wildly between the past and the future, but there is a way to reel the mind back into the present. Through the practice of focused meditation or prayer, we can start to pull the mind back into the present and start living in reality with increased faith and decreased fear. It's not easy, but like everything else we hope to get better at, practice makes progress.

In your daily meditation or prayer time today, think about your focal point. It could be a fixed object a yard or so in front of you. Taking this concept a bit further, your focal point could also be the five to six count breath pattern as you inhale and exhale.

It could even be a word or phrase, like "I am enough." It could be a few meaningful sentences that mean something special to you. Whatever you choose, find your focal point today and know that it will more than likely be challenging to stay focused for very long on the first try. Remember, meditation is a practice. It will take time, just like learning a new skill or learning how to play a new sport or an instrument. On your first try at meditation or prayer, just notice the busyness of your mind and smile and refocus for a few minutes and then the next time, add another minute.

Keep coming back to your focal point, to your breath, to your heartbeat, to the way your body feels in Mountain Pose, and to your intentions for the day. And then, when the mind wanders again, just smile again, knowing this is what the mind does, and refocus on your chosen focal point.

Just like lifting weights, meditating, or praying, it is a practice and a process. Be patient with yourself. The more we lift weights, the stronger we get. Consistency is key. Like weight lifting, results will come with time. As you hone the skill of staying in the present, versus hopping back and forth between the past and the future, you will learn to see things as they are actually happening in front of you, and that awareness will help you create the future you desire. This is easy to say but not easy to do. Our minds are always working, and it is very difficult to sit quietly with ourselves. It is, in fact, one of the most challenging things to do. At the same time, it is one of the most important things to do.

1. Do you feel like the person you are inside is actually what people see daily on the outside? Or do you feel a bit like an imposter in your relationships? If so, what changes would you need to make to become more authentically yourself in relationships that matter to you? Do you think that it's important? If so, could you share a bit of your real self with at least one trusted person? We all have secrets and scars; who could you trust with yours? Who would you share with, and what would you share first?

2. Now consider your partner, spouse, friends, and colleagues. If it's appropriate, what would happen if you checked in with one or more of them this week and asked how things are really going, or how they are really feeling, and then, if there is anything that is challenging for them, would you feel comfortable asking, "How can I help?" Who would those people be, and how do you think they'd respond to that question?

MANIFEST

Set your timer for five more minutes, answer question number two, and consider how you can "show up" differently in your life today to both see and be seen!

1. If appropriate, and only if no harm will come to you or anyone else in the process, identify one thing that you'd like to share with someone that you trust, maybe a family member or a close friend, in order to build a stronger relationship and in order to become the most authentic version of yourself both inside and out.

2. If appropriate, and only if no harm will come to you or anyone else in the process, identify one person in your family, or perhaps a close friend, who you think, or know, may have a lot going on in their lives right now. Plan on how you will reach out to them in order to see how they are actually doing beyond the socially acceptable smile, beyond the "I'm fine, thanks for asking, and how are you?" Some will welcome the concern and care, but others may not. For those that welcome it, perhaps simply ask, "How can I help?"

PRACTICE

The Yoga Mindset in REAL TIME:

Today, or anytime you feel a desire to see and be seen in relationships, take action with the Yoga Mindset in real time!

1. **MOVE:** Inhale slowly for five to six counts and exhale slowly for five to six counts and stand in Mountain Pose. Lift your gaze and softly fix your gaze on a point or object about a yard, or a meter, ahead of you, and quietly repeat to yourself that you have the right to see and be seen with each breath.

2. **MEDITATE:** Declare, "Life is not happening *to* me, life is happening *for* me."

3. **MANIFEST:** Visualize yourself seeing, really seeing others, as they are, and then visualize yourself being seen. What would that look like in your life? Give yourself permission to observe your feelings, the feelings of others, facial expressions, body language, the energy in the space, the temperature of the space, and a myriad of other unspoken factors you can "see" in your relationships today and learn how to trust your intuition on when to "put yourself out there" to be truly seen, knowing full well both the risk of rejection and reward of a deepened relationship. You always have this choice.

Yoga Mindset Principle #6:
I have the right to see and be seen.
The Yoga Mindset Mantra:
Life is not happening *to* me, life is happening *for* me.

Change your mindset, change your life!

123

CHAPTER 7

I Know

"You are a child of God...
...meant to shine, as children do.
...born to make manifest the glory of God..."

Marianne Williamson

Around 1870, my paternal ancestors immigrated to Pennsylvania from Bohemia, in the Czech Republic. My great Czech grandfather and my great German grandmother lived on massive farms on either side of a hill. The story circulated for generations among the families on both sides of the hill is that my grandfather won my grandmother on a bet in a game of poker with her father. They liked each other immensely, and that poker game was not in any way meant to say she was a commodity to be gambled away so lightly. It was simply the easiest and quickest way he could ask for her hand in marriage since he could barely speak English. Fortunately, he had the winning hand, and my great grandfather gave his blessing by agreeing to their marriage when the game was over.

They had eleven children who worked the farm and mostly lived through the roaring 20s, the Great Depression, World War I, World War II and the Korean War. They truly gave all for their country. From those eleven children came my grandfather and his two younger sisters, my dear great aunts, Emma and Caroline. They were the most precious, and feisty, Methodist women who always doted on me and my sister.

They had a genuine love for life, God, country, and others. They walked with God daily in a vibrant and abiding relationship that seemed to give meaning and purpose to everything they did. They served God by serving others through the selfless giving of their time and talents. They volunteered, taught children's church, cared for the poor, visited the sick, and decorated the graves of deceased family members with bouquets of fragrant flowers from their massive garden. They were the salt of the earth, and their goodness flowed deeply into my soul when I visited every summer from the age of nine to twenty-nine.

It was their constant desire and joy to remind me that God created me, delighted in me, and loved me more than anything in the whole world. As a small child, they introduced me to the concept of God in nature on their hundred-acre farm. On every nature walk, they showed me God, in every acorn, giant oak tree, dandelion, and firefly filling up the summer night skies from the swing on the porch of their farmhouse.

Church occurred daily in the garden with every aspect of planting, tending, and harvesting. That was their sermon. God was in every seed that was planted, every tender shoot that would sprout, and every leaf and blossom that would unfurl to the sun and the rain. They would talk of the importance of rooting deep and wide below the ground in order for the plant to stay nourished, supported and to withstand the elements.

Every maturing plant was an example of endurance and determination as it withstood the wind, the rain, the pests, and of course, the ever-present threat of weeds. We checked every day for weeds as they were the little insidious things that got into the root system of the plant and sucked all its moisture and nutrients away. Those small, seemingly harmless weeds had to be dealt with daily, quickly, and thoroughly if we wanted the plants to have a chance of thriving.

The nourishment we received from every fruit and vegetable harvested was a celebration of having done the hard work of tending the garden of our soul and enjoying the fruits of our labor. It was also an opportunity to share the bounty with their neighbors. It was a calling to share our gifts with others in order to nourish the world.

As a child, it was all magic, adventure, and fantastic stories in the garden. Little did I know they were introducing me to the importance of staying connected and communing with God, the ultimate power source and the Creator of everything. I've read about many other religions and don't pretend to have all the answers, but I think there is more. I remain open to the possibility that there is a Divine Creator in the universe. I know those sneaky old ladies thought the same. They were on a mission to spread God's love to all!

According to my sweet aunts, God is a good and loving Father who sent his Son, Jesus, to the world to show us how to love God and love others. From my stepfather, I learned that God was also holy and to be feared. I don't mean "feared," as in a terrified-for-your-life kind of fear, but in the way, you might fear someone, like your mom, when she calls you by your entire birth name even after you've been adopted and your last name was changed years ago. When that happens, you know you are in serious trouble, and out of a healthy sense of self-preservation and respect, you stop whatever you are doing and run to wherever she is currently located. Upon arrival, you drop all attitude and excuses because this time, you can tell she's not fooling around and won't tolerate even a hint of nonsense.

I have a great deal of respect for God, the Creator of everything, including the very breath filling my lungs as I write this. I marvel at the Creator of both the incomprehensible vastness of space and time and the equally intricate universe within the human eyeball. I can't prove any of it, but after decades of reading, praying, and meditating on all of it, I keep coming back to the concept of an intelligent designer. I simply find it hard to believe that everything that exists in the world is just some haphazard random result of an explosion millions of years ago or that we are all just the result of swamp sludge. There just seems to be something a bit bigger, something a bit more intelligent to all of it and to all of us, in my humble opinion. I don't care too much about whether someone is a Protestant or a Catholic. Those are the crumbs of a relationship with the Creator of the Universe. The relationship is what matters most; that, and loving and serving others.

I wandered away from God at various times in my life because I somehow thought I was unworthy or that God was angry with me. I felt more than once that God had given up on me, but that thinking was incorrect. The God that I know intimately is a good and loving father, full of grace and compassion. This God is like a perfect father who never leaves or wanders away from his children. This God is always standing right next to you, waiting for you to turn your face to Him, as a child would look up to their father for love, guidance, and protection. With an earthly father, or guardian, there are usually some consequences when children don't follow their guidance, but that father, or guardian, never stops loving the children. I believe this is what God is like, too. In the same way, every now and then, God may also call you by your full name to get your attention, to get you back on the best path, and to restore intimate connection, as quickly as possible.

Intimate connection with God is actually not about religion; it's about relationship. In the same way that a father and a child might develop a healthy and mutually loving give-and-take relationship, you can also build a relationship with God. God is love, and in the same way that a father loves his child and lives in relationship with the child, I believe that the Creator, God, also desires a relationship with us, but God doesn't force it. It's up to us to make the first move towards divine love. It's a free gift to take or reject. It's your choice.

According to Dr. Larry Crabb, "God's love is perfect. It gives me all I need to stand as a whole person... I can love because I am loved perfectly. And as I love, without fear and self-protection, I edge toward the infinite mindset that doesn't need to hide or win, or blame, but forgives and lives an abundant life of freedom."

Now, not everyone has had a healthy relationship with their father or God, including me. Believe me when I say, "I get it." You may push back hard against this concept of a loving Father if that was you. I wonder if you could catch yourself the next time you push hard against God and as a third unbiased party, imagine stepping away from yourself and just observing without emotion. Notice what is happening and then smile to yourself and say, "Hmmmm, that's interesting." Consider the source of that reaction. Was it another person's issue that overlapped with your life in the name of religion? Could it be that they misunderstood the love of God? If so, consider flipping the script on the story about those negative experiences placing the issue with the other person. How could that affect your spiritual life? Could it open up a new opportunity for a relationship to begin again or to grow deeper with the Divine?

Perhaps you had a great relationship with your earthly father, but you feel like you are such a hot mess that you don't want to bother God. If that is the case, I hate to break it to you, but the Creator of everything who is omnipotent, omniscient, and infinite, already knows all about it and He still loves you.

Maybe you've had a positive relationship with God, but now you are angry about some hardship in your life and are about two seconds away from throwing this book across the room. If that is you, please know that you are not alone. None of us are immune to the storms of life. Some are more treacherous than others.

In the same way that storms, wind, and rain come to everyone's life, to one degree or another, so does growth. Did you know that when the ground is saturated by rain, roots from a tree, or a plant, will grow deeper and wider in the soil below in order to help the tree or plant stay securely grounded? This movement is what creates a massive unseen root structure deep below the ground. The root system's diameter expands under pressure to fully support the wide canopy of the plant or the tree. Applying that same concept to your life, what do you anchor onto when the storms of life slam into you? Do anchor yourself to the physical things of this world that are fleeting, or do you anchor yourself to the spiritual things of God that are eternal? Do you allow the force of the storms of life to help you grow deeper and wider in relationship with the Creator of the Universe, or do you let the storms of life destroy you? You always have that choice.

While it's awful to be hit or caught in a storm, I wonder if you might be able to change your mindset about them? I wonder if you could change your story about the current or past storms of your life and start telling yourself new stories about how they may have made you stronger, grounded you deeper, or grew you taller? Flip the script. Change your mindset, change your life.

If you are really interested in moving forward in your life, no matter what circumstance you are in, and if you feel like you've tried it all and nothing worked, then try plugging in, or back in, to the real power source, the Creator of the Universe. Consider meeting daily, as you would a dear friend, in a relationship. Then, just talk and listen. Watch for the small things that start to happen in your life as a result of connecting to the Divine.

I can really only speak from the point of view of a Christian on the topic of starting a relationship with God, so if you are open to learning more about how to meditate within the Christian faith, check out this ancient Christian meditation practice called Lectio Divina, which is Latin for divine reading. Don't have a bible? No worries. There is an app for that! If possible, download The Bible App. Alternatively, you could just search up any book of the bible online. If technology is not your thing, then try a recycled book store. They always have bibles. The NIV or ESV are easy to read versions. Whatever you select, just make sure you can understand it. When you get to a passage that is hard to understand, use technology for a detailed explanation. Start with the Book of Mark, or the Psalms or Proverbs, as a text to meditate on daily. If you are not a

Christian, then *any* other inspirational book will work. It could be prose, poetry or a novel. There are five steps to the process of divine reading, and freelance writer Elizabeth Manneh laid them out beautifully:

Lectio Divina (Divine Reading for a Daily Meditation Practice)

- **Prepare**

  I'd suggest 30 minutes to read, reflect, and respond to the Holy Spirit's promptings in Lectio Divina. To tune in, I like to light a candle, not because it's necessary, but because the flame and fragrance serve as gentle reminders when collecting my thoughts and calming my mind. I pray a prayer of invitation, saying something like, "God, let me hear from you," and spend a few moments sitting quietly so my mind is open to hearing from God.

- **Read (Lectio)**

  My first reading is an opportunity to get to know the Scripture passage. I listen carefully for any words or phrases that seem to jump out. It's important not to force things but wait patiently for God to give gentle guidance. One day when reading Jeremiah 31, I felt my mind drawn to the strength of God's commitment to His covenant: "[I will make a new covenant] not like the covenant that I made with their fathers on the day when I took them by the hand to bring them out of the land of Egypt, my covenant that they broke, though I was their husband." (Jeremiah 31:32 English Standard Version) I was struck by the image of God leading His people by the hand as an act of love – they weren't left to begin their momentous journey alone.

- **Reflect(Meditatio)**

  The second reading of the same passage focuses further on the points I become aware of during the first reading. Often I'll just re-read a few verses so I can reflect carefully on where God had nudged me. Then I'll reflect on what I believe God is saying, I try not to analyze the passage. It's easy to slip into "study mode" and think about interesting points rather than listening to what God might be saying. It helps to ask God to make his focus clear.

- **Respond (Oratio)**

  After a third reading, it's time to respond. I like to record my thoughts by journaling because I know I'm very prone to forgetting what I've learned, even by the next day! We can respond in prayer too, which gives us the opportunity for a conversation with God. When reading Jeremiah, I journaled my wonderings. If God is so powerfully committed to keeping His covenant with me, why do I sometimes lack the commitment to stay close to God? Often the events of the day crowd in, and I don't always make time to listen to God. I prayed that God would help me to prioritize spending time with Him.

- **Rest (Contemplatio)**

  After the final reading, I spent around 10 minutes in silent contemplation... I just sit quietly and allow God to work. When my mind starts to wander and dart here and there, I bring it gently back to stillness again... It's important to remember that Lectio Divina is not an end in itself or another spiritual practice to tick off our to-do list. It helps us hear specifically and individually from God through Scripture, guided by the Holy Spirit, and deepens our relationship with Him.

If you are meditating on the Bible, it can help you root and grow deeper in a relationship with God, and His love will begin to flow in and through your life. That divine love can empower you to love and serve others. To get that close, though, you have to believe that you are welcome. My dear reader, without a doubt, you are. No matter what you've done, or who you are, all are welcome in the Christian faith. Simply come as you are.

Deepak Chopra summed it up beautifully when he wrote that "All of us need to believe that we are loved and lovable…All of us must discover for ourselves that love is a force as real as gravity and that being upheld in love every day, every hour, every minute, is not a fantasy - it is intended as our natural state. The path to love isn't a choice… this is our spiritual destiny… love reflects God. Jesus always spoke of God as a loving father… a relationship… between parent and child."

When I turned my face back to God, the Divine Creator of everything, in that yoga studio in Singapore, I was whole again. A peace that passes all understanding flowed back into my life and a deep rest that I'd not felt for years settled into my soul. I'd tried to fill that void with so many different things, but nothing ever fully satisfied. Everything else was crumbs. Reconnecting and communing with the Creator of everything was the banquet.

As we moved and breathed, as a class, in that dimly lit yoga studio, at just the right moments, the instructor whispered "presence" in being able to see life as it was actually unfolding in front of us, not as we wished it to be, and "peace," in seeing how everything in our lives was all connected and was working for us. He reminded us of the freedom that could be found in seeing that life was not just happening to us, but for us. In the span of a moment, those words, those thoughts, those revelations, resonated so profoundly in my heart, soul, and mind that it changed my mindset completely.

I remembered again who I was, the place where I began, the place I was now because of all that had happened in my life, and the place where I wanted to be in the future. I saw it all at once. I saw the fragments of my life like that precious bowl that had fallen to the floor, shattered by unanticipated experiences in life. I realized that I'd been operating from a place of disconnectedness, anxiety and overwhelm for years, trying to hold all those broken pieces together and at the same time trying to ignore them. Some call it Imposter Syndrome. I didn't know what it was called. I only knew that I felt broken, and therefore, imperfect. I judged all those cracks and fragments of my life as weaknesses on my part and things not to be discussed.

In that yoga class, however, everything shifted. Instead of the normal mode of critical self-judgment, as the light of the morning started creeping into the studio, I saw those fragments of my life in a new way. With compassion and acceptance, I saw the story each fragment told, and the way it had helped me to grow deeper, stronger, and more resilient.

I felt like every fractured piece, though painfully created, happened perhaps not for a reason, but for an opportunity. An opportunity to grow and live a better version of myself and my life. When I realized that, I sensed the presence of God, and my heart opened. Gordon MacDonald reminds us that "Resilient people open their hearts to the presence of God."

I shifted from a place of shame and fear to a place of love and compassion. The hot mess was still there on the inside, but this time, instead of looking away and diving into one more distraction to avoid dealing with the disconnected fragments of my life, I was fully present and saw things as they actually were, and it was a glorious mess.

I envisioned myself tenderly collecting, inspecting, and listening to the story and lesson of each fragment. I saw myself lovingly gluing the pieces back together, one by one, with lines of precious gold until I was fully restored to my former beauty and stronger than I'd ever been before.

The feeling that I was a hot mess beyond repair, alone, disconnected and separate from everyone and everything evaporated, as the illusion it was, in that moment. Connection with myself, others, and the Divine was restored. I wasn't lost in the past or the future anymore. I was simply present, aware, and seeing things as they were. I was able to see how all the fragments were all connected and happening for me all along. Joy rushed in where pain and suffering had taken root in my heart. Peace settled in where fear and anxiety had gripped my soul for so long. Love replaced the judgment that had been taking up so much space in my mind. Heart, soul, and mind, I had made it to the top of the mountain.

I was standing firm, rooted, aligned, integrated, and resilient, with my leg strong, my pelvis neutral, my core sealed, my heart open, my voice resonating, and my eyes focused on what was unfolding all around me. My thoughts were lifted towards the heavens, and my spirit was communing with the Divine. The perfect love of God was there. "When that love is known and felt by us, it affects how we view ourselves and ultimately, how we view one another. God's love for us results in a proper love for ourselves and then extends to love for our neighbors," according to James Bryan Smith.

At that summit, the view was breathtaking. Feeling the fullness of God's perfect love flowing through me again, I looked down the mountain and saw how it all fit together. At the very bottom, I was a child, back in my Aunt's garden.

I saw myself like a small seed planted deep in the soil of God's perfect love. I saw the tender stem of my life rising up, so fragile, but growing stronger with every life storm. I saw my life open up like a thousand perfectly imperfect fragmented petals, lined with the most precious gold and reflecting God's love and light into the world.

Like the Samurai warrior, seeing the gold running throughout and telling its thousand fragment story, I was very pleased. Feeling that joy rising up inside me, a smile spread across my lips as the class came to a close, and the teacher asked us to stand together in Mountain Pose with hands in prayer position at our hearts once more.

I grounded my feet and thought, *I am, and I have the right to be here.*

I brought my pelvis to neutral and thought, *I feel, both physically and emotionally.*

I sealed my core and thought, *I do, and I have the right to set and accomplish my goals.*

I lifted my heart and thought, *I love, and I have the right to give and receive love.*

I inhaled deeply and thought, *I speak, and I have the right to speak and be heard.*

I chose a focal point and thought, *I see, and I have the right to see and be seen.*

I lifted my face to God and thought, *I know, and I have the right to know and be known by God.*

With my hands to my heart and eyes closed, I bowed to the Yoga Instructor and whispered "*Namaste*," which means, loosely, "The light in me sees, and honors, the light in you."

The Yoga Mindset Formula, Day 7

MOVE

**Mountain Pose Alignment Principle #7: Lift the head!
Set your timer for 5 minutes and move!**

The Head & Breathwork

1. Set the foundation by moving feet hip width apart and toes forward. Move the shins forward, thighs back, keep the legs strong, and stand tall. Add that knee-saving micro bend, bring the pelvis to a neutral position, seal the core, rotate the triceps towards the back and the palms forward slightly. Hug the shoulder blades towards the spine and down, open your chest and lift your heart. Lift your gaze to look straight ahead, with the jawline pulled back, ears over shoulders, and head in line with the spine, find a focal point about a meter or more in front of you. Fix your eyes softly on that spot. Inhale for five to six slow counts as you sweep your arms up over your head, pause for five to six slow counts at the top of your inhale, then sweep your arms down to your sides as you exhale for five to six slow counts and pause at the bottom of your exhale for five to six counts.

2. As you slowly inhale and exhale three to six times, quietly repeat to yourself, "I have the right to know and be known." Focus on lifting the head up a little higher, and as you do, consider your relationship with the Creator of the Universe. The Creator knows you and desires to be in relationship with you. You can tap into the power of the Divine by simply speaking to God as

you would another person. Imagine God, a good and loving parent who wants only the best for you. Let that unconditional love flow into you, healing and empowering you to love God, others and yourself supernaturally as you move through your day today.

MEDITATE

Take a seat, set your timer for five minutes, and answer questions seven and eight. Come back later to answer the other questions as time permits.

1. What has your experience with God been like in your life?
2. Do you believe in God, or some version of a God, or a Creator of everything?
3. Do you believe that God wants to know you intimately in a relationship?
4. Do you tend to keep communication one way, or do you try to listen to the gentle whispers of God, too?
5. Are you afraid of an intimate relationship with the Divine? Why or why not?
6. What is one thing you can do today to deepen your connection with the Creator of everything?
7. Can you think of one to three experiences that have negatively impacted your relationship with God?
8. Can you write out at least one positive result that may have come from those experiences?

MANIFEST

Set your timer for five more minutes and answer question number two. Come back later to answer question number one as time permits.

1. Consider the concept of the Creator of everything. Then imagine that Creator as the most perfect parent who loves you unconditionally and longs to be in relationship with you and only wants the very best for you. Can you receive that love and lift up some words or a prayer of gratitude? Why or why not?

2. Next, see yourself as free from fear and judgment in the relationship and consider how you can "show up" in relationship with the Infinite God differently this week. Can you share what you hope for yourself and for others with God and then listen for the soft whisper of the divine in your life in reply, knowing that it's not always going to be a yes? Even an earthly father knows better than to give their kids everything they want. Sometimes things like candy are harmful, and sometimes, not getting everything you want is a stroke of luck.

PRACTICE

The Yoga Mindset in REAL TIME

Today, or anytime you desire to grow deeper in relationship with God, take action with the Yoga Mindset in real time.

1. **MOVE:** Inhale slowly for five to six counts and then exhale slowly for five to six counts while standing in Mountain Pose with the top of your head reaching up to the heavens and remembering that you have the right to know and be known by God.

2. **MEDITATE:** Declare, "Life is not happening *to* me, life is happening *for* me."

3. **MANIFEST:** Visualize yourself in an intimate relationship with God, the Creator of everything. What would that look like in your life? Let yourself feel it. How could that relationship change your life? How can you make that a reality?

Yoga Mindset Principle #7:
I have the right to know and be known.
The Yoga Mindset Mantra:
Life is not happening *to* me, life is happening *for* me.

Change your mindset, change your life!

CHAPTER 8

We Are

*"One day
when I was sitting quiet...
it came to me:
that feeling of being part of everything,
not separate at all..."*

The Color Purple, *by Alice Walker*

Congratulations! You made it to the top of the mountain!

How's the view? Hopefully, you are enjoying a new and spectacular view from the proverbial mountaintop. Can you also look down to the base of your personal mountain journey and "see" all the stops that you made along the path? Can you see the various fragments of your life at each stop? Can you visualize how those fragments might be lovingly collected and connected with lines of gold, telling their stories? Can you look over all of it, seeing the light of the sun reflecting off of the lines of gold, and like the Samurai warrior in the opening story of the book, say that you are pleased? If so, you have truly reached the top of the mountain. If not, no judgement. This is a lifetime journey. Take time to go back to an area where you still feel stuck. Do the work of going through the questions for reflection. Eventually, there will be a breakthrough.

If this journey was beneficial for you, good news: There is more! Now, you can move forward, as you are, perfectly imperfect, with all the cracks of your life on display in lines of gold telling their story for all to see. Your confidence to be your real self, scars and all, and to speak about those scars lined with gold, may start to help others. That will be your opportunity to be courageous and share your story about how you weathered the storm and flipped the script. It will be your opportunity to speak hope into the seemingly impossible and to guide them on a journey up their personal mountain, too.

You have a role to play. You were born for a reason, and a purpose, and you have work to do in the short amount of time you've been given on this earth. As Albert Schwitzer said, "I don't know what your destiny will be, but one thing I know: The only ones among you who will really be happy are those who have sought and found how to serve."

There are so many other people in the world who need to know that they are not alone in whatever battle they are facing. We are all kintsugi, and we are all connected, and the journey up and down the mountain never actually ends for any of us. We are all just at different points on the mountain at different times in our lives. We'll continue to go up and down the mountain, and in and out of the seven life alignment principles, to adjust constantly, and readjust or connect another fragment of our life to our story over the course of our lives.

The storms of life will still come, on that you can depend, but now you can also depend on the Yoga Mindset Formula and Mountain Pose to help you stand your ground and stand tall, integrated and resilient.

It's not the storm that breaks you. It's never been about the storm. It's always been about your reaction to the storm. It's always been about your mindset. So, keep The Yoga Mindset with you wherever you go and start living your best life now.

MOVE: Inhale for five to six slow counts and exhale for five to six slow counts. Repeat one to three times, and stand grounded, integrated, and resilient in Mountain Pose.

MEDITATE: Declare "Life is not happening TO me. Life is happening FOR me." Look for the positive lessons in every situation and tell yourself a new, better, and empowering story.

MANIFEST: Visualize the life you want, rewire your mind to create that better future for yourself, let the words of your vision echo softly into the universe, then make a plan and start taking action. See it in your mind's eye. Feel it as a reality. What would your life look like? Free yourself to move forward towards the best version of your life as you define it.

Change your mindset, change your life!

You are the author of your life story, but it may not happen the way you envision it if you don't write the script. You have the power to dream and imagine and reach out for help and support to get there. It all starts with a breath, a thought, and then an action. It starts with moving, meditating, and manifesting. It starts with the Yoga Mindset.

Choose how you will show up for your life, intentionally, every day from this day forward. Learn the lessons from the storms and the cracks in your life. Mend those cracks with precious lines of gold and start living your life to the fullest as a perfectly imperfect vessel.

Let your life be a spectacular skyscraper firmly anchored into a massive, level, and stable foundation deep beneath the earth. See your life soaring to the heavens in communion with the Divine. Make your life a masterpiece. Let it inspire others. Let it be a breathtaking mosaic life, telling its story in lines of gold.

It will take great courage to display and talk about those lines of gold in your life, but it is the very thing that can free you up and propel you forward to the best version of yourself and your life as you envision it. There is great power in your story. Embrace it. Celebrate it. Share it. Use it to lift others up. You have a purpose to fulfill in the very short amount of time you've been given. There is nothing more important.

Next Steps!

Now that you have had a small taste of the power of changing your life through The Yoga Mindset, keep going! Prioritize your health, take care of your body, go deeper into the seven alignment secrets, learn how to apply those alignment principles not only to every other yoga pose you hope to master, but also your life on a daily basis. Move, meditate and manifest the best version of yourself and your life in real time with me in a FREE 3-Day Yoga Mindset Group Challenge. To join this challenge, click here: www.mosaicconcepts.com/yogachallenge

The FREE 3 Day Yoga Mindset Challenge includes:

- 3 - Yoga Anatomy & Alignment Sessions
- 3 - Yoga Mindset Sessions
- 3 - 15 minute Yoga Sessions

If you have any questions about these additional options, or you are ready to sign up for one of this additional options, schedule a FREE 1 on 1 consultation call with me, or my team, here:

https://calendly.com/mosaicconcepts-coachmichelle

Take the next step. Make The Yoga Mindset a way of life. Ground yourself in this 15 minute daily mindfulness practice, so that you can rise up, reach out and move forward in your life with passion, power and purpose. Connect with The Yoga Mindset tribe. Come together as the spectacular mosaic of people that you are, from all around the world to move, meditate and manifest the best version of yourself and your life as you envision it together.

Thank you so much for practicing extravagant self-care by joining me on this journey through The Yoga Mindset. I hope that it was all that you hoped for, that you made it to the top of your epic mountain of a life (or are at least getting closer to the summit) and that the view was life-changing for you, too.

Remember, it's a lifetime journey of going up and down that mountain and revising your intentions for your life. Remember that moment when you caught a glimpse of that view of your best self and your best life. Set aside 15 minutes every day and reconnect with yourself and that vision every morning with The Yoga Mindset Formula. Experience that vision for your life with all your senses and then do the work of making your dreams a reality by taking action. Harness the force of the storms of life to your advantage and your chosen destination. Look for the ways life is working for you and then celebrate them. Keep flipping the script on those storms of life and the stories you tell yourself about them. It's all in how you look at it. Change your mindset, change your life.

As the author of your life story, the pen is always in your hand. You get to choose your life story. What new stories will you write? Another way to think about it is to ask yourself what you'd want people to say about you at your funeral or in a memorial article. Now, that changes things up a bit, doesn't it? Time is short, my dear reader. Make the most of it. Make your life a masterpiece. The sky's the limit and that means the options are infinite!

As you continue your personal journey through this crazy amazing world, my wish for you is a loving-kindness meditation that my yoga mentors often speak over me and their other yoga students at the end of a practice. Read it out loud three times, slowly, and let it sink into your heart, soul and mind: May you be safe, may you be healthy, may you be happy and may you walk through the world with ease. Namaste.

Change your mindset, change your life!

DOWNLOAD YOUR FREE GIFTS

Read This First

Just to say thanks for buying and reading my book, I would like to give you three bonus gifts for FREE, no strings attached!

To Download Your 3 FREE BONUS YOGA GIFTS Now, Visit:
www.TheYogaMindsetBook.com/FreeGifts

I appreciate your interest in my book, and I value your feedback as it helps me improve future versions of this book. I would appreciate it if you could leave your invaluable review on Amazon.com with your feedback. Thank you!

References

Carr, Kris, "*It's not about finding your voice…,*" https://kriscarr.com/

Carrey, Jim, (November 2017), "*Life doesn't happen to you, it happens for you,*" Retrieved from YouTube Full Speech: Jim Carrey's Commencement Address at the Maharishi International University @ https://www.youtube.com/watch?v=koLqxXcuq3s

Catron, Mandy Len, (2015, August), *Falling in Love is the Easy Part*, https://www.ted.com/talks/mandy_len_catron_falling_in_love_is_the_easy_part

Chapman, Gary, *The 5 Love Languages*, Northfield Publishing, 2010

Chopra, Deepak, *The Path to Love*, Harmony Books, 1997

Cloud, Henry Dr., *9 Things You Simply Must Do*, Integrity Publishers, 2004

Cushnir, Raphael, *Setting Your Heart on Fire*, Broadway Books, 2003

Davis, Pam, *Kintsugi: The Value of a Broken Bowl*, The Younique Foundation

Dickens, Charles, *A Tale of Two Cities*, Ino Editions, 2018

Downing, Jim, *Meditation*, NavPress, 2011

Farris, Jon Val, "*From Broken to Beautiful: The Power of Kintsugi,*" HuffPost Contributor Platform, December 2017

Gates, Rolf, *Meditations on Intention and Being*, Anchor Books, December 2015

Gawain, Shakti, *Creative Visualization*, Nataraj Publishing, 2002

Hensel, Gary, *I Am,* Balboa Printing, December 2016

Hood, Katie (2019, June), *The Difference Between Healthy and Unhealthy Love*, Retrieved from Ted Talks at https://www.youtube.com/watch?v=ON4iy8hq2hM

Jacobsen, Wayne, *The Vineyard*, Harvest House, 1992

Judith, Anodea, *Chakra Balancing*, Sounds True Publishing, 2003

Leatherbury, Hannah, *5 Yoga Practices to Balance the Throat Chakra,* Retrieved at yogiapproved.com at *https://www.yogiapproved.com/om/throat-chakra-healing-yoga-practices/*

Lindberg, Anne Morrow, Gift of the Sea, Pantheon Publishing, 1991

MacDonald, Gordon, *Ordering Your Private World*, Thomas Nelson Publishing, 1985

Menneh, Elizabeth (2020 March), *Lectio Divina: A Beginner's Guide,* Retrieved from Busted Halo, https://bustedhalo.com/ministry-resources/lectio-divina-beginners-guide

Moore, Catherine, *Positive Daily Affirmations: Is There Science Behind It?,* Retrieved from PositivePsychology.com at https://positivepsychology.com/daily-affirmations/

Myers, Thomas W., *Anatomy Trains*, Churchill Livingstone, February 2014

Myss, Caroline, *Anatomy of the Spirit*, Three Rivers Press, 1996

Neruda, Pablo, *Love Sonnet XI*, Retrieved from PoetryAnalysis.com at https://www.pablonerudapoems.com/sonnet-xi/

Nestor, James, *Breathe*, Riverhead Books, 2020

Robbins, Mel, *The Five Second Rule*, Savio Republic Publishing, 2017

Ruiz, Don Miguel, *The Four Agreements*, Amber-Allen Publishing, 1997

Schwitzer, Albert, *"I don't know what your destiny will be…,"* Goodreads

Sinek, Simon, *What's the Best Way to Confront Someone*, Retrieved from YouTube Video at https://www.youtube.com/watch?v=dCkxgICCVWU

Smith, James Bryan, *Embracing the Love of God*, Harper Collins San Francisco

Smith, Kathy, *How to Actually Practice Mountain Pose – There's More Technique Than You Think*, www.yogiapproved.com,

Thich, Nhat Hanh, *Please Call Me by My True Names*, Retrieved plumvillage.org at https://plumvillage.org/articles/please-call-me-by-my-true-names-song-poem/

Walker, Alice, *The Color Purple*, Pocket Publishing, March 1987

Williamson, Marianne, *Our Deepest Fear*, 1996, https://poemanalysis.com/marianne-williamson/our-deepest-fear/

Yax, John & Chris, Yax Yoga Concepts and The Complete Posture Blueprint, www.yaxyogaconcepts.com

Acknowledgments

I had no idea how many people it takes to create a book! There is no way to acknowledge them all, but I'd like to give credit to a few...

To the first, best, and most creative author, who, with just a breath, spoke everything in this magical and mysterious universe into being. It is a delight to know and walk closely with you.

To Cris Cawley, CEO of Game Changer Publishing, and her amazing Publishing Crew, thank you for your outstanding wisdom and guidance on every detail from the thousand foot viewpoint.

To Ms. Alyea, my ninth grade English Teacher, thank you for noticing my first efforts at writing and for sparking the flame for language arts deep inside of me.

To the Yax Yoga Brothers, John and Chris, thank you for teaching from the heart, for the gift of your knowledge, and for de-mystifying yoga just enough so that it was finally and fully accessible, and then re-mystifying just enough so that it remained fully magic and intoxicating mystery.

To all the inspirational authors, and their books decorating so many of the walls and corners of my home, thank you, thank you, thank you for sucking the marrow out of life so that we might live: Maya Angelou's *I Know Why the Caged Bird Sings*, Jane Austen's *Pride and Prejudice*, Corrie Ten Boom's *The Hiding Place*, Geraldine Brooks' *Year of Wonder* and *March*, Elizabeth Barrett Browning's *Selected Poems*, Pat Conroy's *Beach Music,* Charles Dickens' *A Tale of Two Cities*, Kristen Hannah's *The*

Nightingale, O. Henry's *The Gift of the Magi*, James Hilton's *Lost Horizon*, C.S. Lewis' *The Lion, The Witch and The Wardrobe*, Anne Morrow Lindbergh's *The Gift of the Sea*, John Steinbeck's *The Grapes of Wrath*, J.R.R. Tolkien's *Lord of the Rings Trilogy*, to name a few.

To my parents, you made it! We made it! Thank you for agreeing to celebrate the lines of gold in your life in the hopes that it might help even just one person.

To my brilliant husband, Dan, thank you for being an eternal optimist and for always reminding me how to eat this proverbial elephant of a book - one bite at a time. Organization really is your superpower!

Last but not least, to my three wonderful children, thank you for going solo for months when I was MIA while writing this book. #mykidsare-adulting! I love you, I love you more…INFINITY!

Made in the USA
Las Vegas, NV
07 January 2024

84009183R00098